"This reader-friendly book is a masterful guide fo[...] ness and humility, *Mindful Discipline* weaves toge[...] wisdom of reflection, and decades of clinical expe[...] the most exceptional road maps on how to raise happy, resilient, and emotionally healthy children."

—**Andrew Weil, MD**, author of *Spontaneous Happiness* and *Eight Weeks to Optimum Health*

"If you raise your children with respect for who they are, nourishing compassion, clarity, and wise limits, they will bloom and blossom. The tools for mindfully doing so are here in these pages."

—**Jack Kornfield, PhD**, author of *A Path with Heart*

"I'm deeply impressed and inspired by what [Shapiro and White] are offering the world! It fills such an essential niche, and moves forward our understanding of 'how to' in an important way."

—**Tara Brach, PhD**, author of *Radical Acceptance* and *True Refuge*

"This intelligent, tender, and beautifully written book helps parents tap into their inner wisdom and create the optimal emotional environment for their child's growth and development. Loaded with powerful exercises grounded in clinical expertise and scientific theory, this book will help all of us navigate the path of parenting with greater ease, clarity, and grace."

—**Kristin Neff, PhD**, associate professor of human development and culture at the University of Texas at Austin and author of *Self-Compassion*

"Coming from an expert on mindfulness and a leading pediatrician, this deeply wise book shows parents how to nourish both self-discipline and self-worth inside the children they love. Grounded in research, full of personal examples, and loaded with down-to-earth suggestions, this book is a gem."

—**Rick Hanson, PhD**, author of *Hardwiring Happiness*

"*Mindful Discipline* should be read by every parent. This book contains the operating instructions for family life that none of us received in school. Twenty-five years ago mindfulness saved my life. Now it informs all of my actions, including the way I am with my children."

—**Noah Levine**, author of *Dharma Punx* and *Refuge Recovery*

"Shauna Shapiro and Chris White have created a wonderful integration of the power of mindful awareness and the insights from studies of child development and the brain to lovingly guide us to a more rewarding and effective way of being as parents. The science of attachment reveals that the most robust predictor of our child's development is how we have come to make sense of our lives from the inside out. This book beautifully illuminates how the previously independent fields of attachment and of mindfulness actually share common ground—that knowing yourself is the best gift you can give to your children. An effective way of achieving this parental presence is through mindfulness, and the stories, ideas, and exercises of *Mindful Discipline* offer a fabulous guide to creating the deep and receptive internal knowing that will empower your children to become resilient, reflective, and compassionate beings themselves. What better gift can you offer of yourself to your child, and the world?"

> —**Daniel J. Siegel, MD**, clinical professor at the University of California, Los Angeles, school of medicine; author of *Brainstorm* and *The Mindful Brain*; and coauthor of *No-Drama Discipline*, *Parenting from the Inside Out*, and *The Whole-Brain Child*

"This finely and sensitively written book points to the fragility and resilience of a child's soul and demonstrates so clearly how in need each child is of an equally fragile and resilient adult's guidance. An adult, however, having been on the Earth much longer, has been able to add experience to the fragility and resilience and thus becomes the author of the child's life until he or she is experienced enough to become the author himself or herself. This beautiful book is a wonderful guide to parents who wish to lovingly, mindfully, and clearly accompany their children at the beginning of their life journey."

> —**Meinir Davies**, management and teaching team coordinator at the New Village School, Sausalito, CA

"*Mindful Discipline* is the perfect guide for conscious parents and teachers. Grounded in solid neuroscience, it shows how to be loving and remain centered, while teaching children to develop their own internal wisdom and good hearts. This book is a gift!"

> —**James Baraz**, cofounder of Spirit Rock Meditation Center and coauthor of *Awakening Joy: 10 Steps to Happiness*

"*Mindful Discipline* is an intelligent and creative approach to the omnipresent challenge of parenting: how to be kind and loving yet firm and in control. I was struck by the multiple levels of authority the authors drew upon: deep scholarship, personal struggles with parenting, and hard-earned meditative insight."

> —**Fred Luskin, PhD**, director of the Stanford Forgiveness Project and author of *Forgive for Good*

"The wonderful, authoritative, generous, and warm-hearted guidance offered by these two skilled parents, educators, and researchers confirms that the medium is indeed the message. This book, unique in a world of instruction manuals, engages, encourages, and inspires parents both old and new to trust their own inherent goodness and kindness to connect with the impulse to flourish that is part of every child's potential, so that parenting and growing up—the most basic of experiences—become a sacred joy! What a treasure this book will be to so many people!"

—**Sylvia Boorstein**, author of *Happiness Is an Inside Job: Practicing for a Joyful Life*

"From the opening pages, *Mindful Discipline* is practical, authentic, and compassionate. The authors simultaneously support our deepest desires as parents and acknowledge the messy realities of parenting. They offer guiding principles, specific practices, and, most importantly, heartfelt compassion for all of us engaged in the moment-to-moment process of creating healthy, loving relationships with our children. This book is a valuable resource for me personally, and for the parents, children, and families I serve."

—**Amy Saltzman MD**, author of *A Still Quiet Place*

"Drawing from their own experience as parents, plus many great teachers of our time, White and Shapiro give us invaluable insights and personal practices to understand and embody the process of parenting in order to raise loving, conscious humans. This in-depth and thoughtful book weaves the principles of parenting with precise instructions for self-inquiry so that both parent and child thrive in the relationship."

—**Lindy Woodard, MD**, Pediatric Alternatives, Mill Valley, CA

"The wisdom in this book rings true for me on so many levels—as a psychologist, scientist, mindfulness scholar, and most of all, a parent. In a gentle and accessible manner, Shapiro and White use both science and wisdom to explain exactly how to hold firm boundaries and loving limits while being authentic, present, and compassionate—blending these ingredients into a recipe for creating a harmonious home and being the kind of parent all of us aspire to be."

—**Cassandra Vieten, PhD**, president of the Institute of Noetic Sciences and author of *Mindful Motherhood*

"Whether parents have an established mindfulness practice or are new to this ancient wisdom, *Mindful Discipline* readers will gain a fresh and confident approach to parenting and a life based in mindfulness. This book's easy-to-read chapters offer valuable parenting advice rooted in psychology and practical exercises readers can use to take their parenting to the next level."

—**Sarah Wood Vallely,** author of *Sensational Meditation for Children*

"Are you tired of using discipline techniques that strain your parent-child relationship and only offer short-term results? *Mindful Discipline* is an insightful and inspiring book designed to help parents respond calmly and thoughtfully to behavior challenges, and provide the love, guidance, and appropriate boundaries children need. Shauna Shapiro and Chris White show us how a mindful awareness practice, along with the essential elements of *Mindful Discipline*, can lead to self-growth, deeper connection with our children, and a greater understanding of children's underlying needs."

—**Katie Vasicek, MA**, parent coach (www.vistaparenting.com)

"Parenting may be the most difficult job on the planet. It also may be the most joyful and rewarding thing a person can do. Shapiro and White have drawn upon science, theory, and their deep well of experience to craft a practical and meaningful guide for fostering the growth of loving, emotionally intelligent, and responsible children. I am certain that parents who put into practice the wisdom found in *Mindful Discipline* will be offering a blessing to their child for life."

—**Steven D. Hickman, PsyD**, clinical psychologist and executive
    director at the University of California, San Diego's Center for
    Mindfulness

"Beautifully written. *Mindful Discipline* puts the research-validated elements of good parenting—loving unconditionally, supporting autonomy, mentoring healthy habits, setting healthy boundaries, and reframing mistakes as learning opportunities—into the context of conscious and compassionate coaching, teaching parents to guide children in their natural developmental trajectory from impulse to judgment to responsibility. Shapiro and White offer simple, practical tools that develop the capacities of emotional intelligence, resilience, and self-discipline that grow an authentic inner compass of responsibility and integrity for both parent and child. I'm recommending the book wholeheartedly to every parent and parent-to-be; it's a masterful gem."

—**Linda Graham, MFT**, author of *Bouncing Back: Rewiring Your Brain
    for Maximum Resilience and Well-Being*

"Who doesn't want independent and loving children? In *Mindful Discipline*, Shapiro and White provide us with principles and tools to create a harmonious family life and self-disciplined children."

> —**Victoria Maizes, MD**, executive director at the Arizona Center for Integrative Medicine and author of *Be Fruitful: The Essential Guide to Maximizing Fertility and Giving Birth to a Healthy Child*

"Sigmund Freud called parenting 'an impossible profession.' In the midst of our self-help culture's overly simple solutions to the complex challenges of contemporary lives, *Mindful Discipline* speaks to those facing this impossible task with kindness, deep wisdom, and refreshing sanity. Digesting the essence of the latest research and theory, it also clearly sees the messy living rooms of contemporary parents aspiring to bring their highest consciousness to the sometimes exhausting daily realities of parenting. It invites you to always keep growing, as best you can, together with your kids. Your family will never be perfect, but your mindfulness, and your emotional intelligence, can always be developing. That's real; and it's more than enough to give your kids what they really need, especially when fueled by the compassion and wisdom you'll contact in these pages.

> —**Terry Patten**, senior author, with Ken Wilber, of *Integral Spiritual Practice*

"Drawing from their own experience as parents, plus many great teachers of our time, Shapiro and White give us invaluable insights and personal practices to understand and embody the process of parenting in order to raise loving, conscious humans. This in-depth and thoughtful book weaves the principles of parenting with precise instructions for self-inquiry so that both parent and child thrive in the relationship."

> —**Lindy Woodard, MD**, pediatrician and mother of two

"We all know that parenting is wonderful, difficult, mysterious, and challenging. This skillfully crafted book offers an insightful view of parenting as an opportunity to practice mindfulness and awareness. You will find helpful and accessible practices for cultivating clarity, compassion, and resilience for both parent and child. There are many gems, like reframing mistakes to 'mis-takes'— a great gift."

> —**Wendy Palmer**, author of *The Intuitive Body: Discovering the Wisdom of Conscious Embodiment and Aikido*

"If discipline in the home is important to you, *Mindful Discipline* is a must-read! Combining real-life examples with plenty of research-based concepts, authors Shapiro and White make a clear distinction between healthy and unhealthy discipline. They also offer a variety of tools and techniques to help you practice healthy, loving discipline while avoiding its unhealthy forms. It is rare to find a book on discipline that places so much emphasis on the heart of the parent-child relationship."

—**Scott Noelle**, author of *The Daily Groove: How to Enjoy Parenting ... Unconditionally!*

"*Mindful Discipline* offers invaluable insights into the dynamics of child-and-parent relationships, as well as student-and-learning-companion relationships. Shapiro and White's profound understanding of children's needs perfectly complements the child-centered education of the New Learning Culture approach. It's a must-read for all who aim to be loving mentors for their kids and students."

—**Carmen Gamper**, founder of New Learning Culture

"Shapiro and White's book is an extraordinary resource that will transform the way parents think. *Mindful Discipline* empowers parents and children, striking the perfect balance between love and limits. The explanatory research and hands-on, practical strategies offer a masterful guide to parenting through mindfulness."

—**Laura L. Ellingson**, coauthor (with Patricia Sotirin) of *Aunting: Cultural Practices that Sustain Family and Community Life*

"A rich and wonderful book on how to nourish strength, integrity, and character in one's children; the authors have made a truly important contribution for all those who love their children."

—**Joan Halifax, PhD**, Abbot Upaya Zen Center

"Shapiro and White weave a tapestry of ancient wisdom and current developmental knowledge to give us a gentle guide to becoming the loving parents our children need when it counts the most."

—**Gordon Neufeld, PhD**

"This is a jewel of a book that contains priceless pearls of wisdom. Shapiro and White have written a wonderfully clear and inspiring guide to raising healthy, happy, and emotionally intelligent children. Drawing on the practice of mindfulness and contemporary scientific research, *Mindful Discipline* is filled with expert guidance, experiential practices, and personal stories that masterfully illuminate the way. Every parent should read this book!"

—**Mark Coleman**, author of *Awake in the Wild*

"What an insightful book! With its focus on attitudes, approaches, and intuition rather than on strict rules, children brought up with *Mindful Discipline* are bound to find a harmonious balance between head and heart, strength and softness, curiosity and safety. I love it!"

—**Peter Baumann**, founder of Being Human

"How fortunate parents are to have this courageous and much needed perspective on nurturing their children so that they may grow up to be happy, resilient, and emotionally intelligent adults who are able to work with life's inevitable challenges—and how fortunate children are to have parents who might be guided by the words of wisdom written here! Synthesizing contemporary understanding about what children truly need and mindfulness practices for nurturing love and connection, Shapiro and White have written a clear and fundamentally kind book that encourages parents to trust themselves and their children in the ever-evolving process of growing and learning together, moment-by-moment."

—**Nancy Bardacke**, midwife, mindfulness teacher, and author of *Mindful Birthing: Training the Mind, Body and Heart for Childbirth and Beyond*

"*Mindful Discipline* is an interesting, encouraging, and enlightening contribution to the library of books on parenting. I really appreciate its focus on relationships, starting with a foundation of parental self-discovery and self-discipline. The concepts are thought provoking and the applications and examples are sound and effective. Children and parents will find mutual respect, learning, and joy from this approach, with all parties growing and developing into happier individuals and better citizens. I congratulate the authors on their good work!"

—**Chet D. Johnson, MD, FAAP**, professor of pediatrics and associate director for the Center for Child Health and Development, University of Kansas School of Medicine

"Kids need discipline. While that may be conventional thinking in parenting, it doesn't tell the whole story. Living in an age of distraction and chronic stress, we are raising children with more screen time, less face-to-face time, more control, less connection, more anxiety, less peace and joy, and more punishment with less discipline. *Mindful Discipline* shines a compassionate light on why true discipline is not punitive, but intuitive—not controlling but rooted in healthy connection, and shows us why parenting our children to thrive is about honoring the purpose of your relationship: to grow together. If mindfulness is the heart's discipline, to pay attention, to notice, to connect inside our storms and repair our ruptures, then, we are, in effect, creating a discipline of the heart, and in so doing, we revitalize the heart of healthy family because we understand the truth about what kids—and we—truly need to thrive. An important book."

—**Lu Hanessian**, award-winning writer; author of *Let the Baby Drive* and *The Garden: A Parenting Parable*; former NBC and Discovery Health Channel anchor; parent educator; speaker; and founder of Parent2ParentU.com and WYSH (Wear Your Spirit for Humanity)

mindful discipline

a loving approach to setting limits & raising an emotionally intelligent child

Shauna Shapiro, PhD
Chris White, MD

New Harbinger Publications, Inc.

Publisher's Note

This publication is designed to provide accurate and authoritative information in regard to the subject matter covered. It is sold with the understanding that the publisher is not engaged in rendering psychological, financial, legal, or other professional services. If expert assistance or counseling is needed, the services of a competent professional should be sought.

"It Felt Love" from the Penguin publication THE GIFT: POEMS BY HAFIZ, translated by Daniel Ladinsky. Copyright © 1999 Daniel Ladinsky and used with his permission.

Lyrics from "No One Said It Would Be Easy" by Cloud Cult, written by Craig Minowa. Copyright © 2008 Craig Minowa / Earthology Records. Reprinted with permission.

Excerpt from William Stafford's "You and Art" from THE WAY IT IS: NEW AND SELECTED POEMS. Copyright © 1986, 1998 by William Stafford and the Estate of William Stafford. Reprinted with the permission of The Permissions Company, Inc. on behalf of Graywolf Press, Minneapolis, Minnesota, http://www.graywolfpress.org.

Distributed in Canada by Raincoast Books

Cover design by Amy Shoup
Acquired by Tesilya Hanauer
Edited by Clancy Drake

Library of Congress Cataloging-in-Publication Data on file

Printed in the United States of America

16   15   14

10   9   8   7   6   5   4   3   2   1   First printing

For my son, Jackson Ki

—SS

To mom and dad, who delighted in me from day one

—CW

Parenting is one of the most challenging, demanding, and stressful jobs on the planet. It is also one of the most important, for how it is done influences in great measure the heart and soul and consciousness of the next generation, their experience of meaning and connection, their repertoire of life skills, and their deepest feelings about themselves and their possible place in a rapidly changing world.

—Jon Kabat-Zinn, *Everyday Blessings*

CONTENTS

Appendices

FOREWORD

by Christine Carter, PhD

Are you happy all the time? Do you ever yell at your kids? Because I write and speak professionally about raising happy kids, these are questions that parents ask me all the time. Here's the answer: No, I don't even try to be happy all the time. My goal is to be mindful as much of the time as possible. And yes, I do yell at my kids sometimes—but only when I'm not parenting mindfully.

Synthesizing ancient insights from the East with modern science and psychological knowledge, psychologist and mindfulness expert Shauna Shapiro and pediatrician Chris White have created a beautifully clear, comprehensive, and practical guide to the type of mindful parenting that I recommend parents practice (and that I try to practice myself). *Mindful Discipline* is a step-by-step guide to parenting with greater wisdom and compassion. Think of it as an invitation to use the focus of your mind, and the compassionate love in your heart, to raise happy children and find greater joy in your parenting.

As parents we want nothing more than to help our children grow into their best and brightest selves, to persevere in the pursuit of their dreams, and to be good and decent people who want to make the world a better place. But what do they need from us in order to get there?

There is a mountain of information out there about how best to parent. Some approaches make discipline the central issue but espouse harsh, intimidating, and controlling methods to keep the child in line. In reaction to this authoritarian approach, others have said that children need no limits at all, that discipline is a dirty word that need not be uttered around children. This permissive approach claims we should leave them be and they will grow up to be kind and responsible. But both permissive and authoritarian approaches misunderstand what true discipline is and how it develops. This book clarifies what healthy self-discipline is and why it is important, and it outlines the essential forms of nourishment that help children develop it.

Drawing on modern science, Shapiro and White reveal that children need a healthy combination of love and limits, and that discipline is a necessary ingredient for children to develop the essential capacities of self-regulation, impulse control, and social competence. They invite us as parents to rethink our definition of discipline, reminding us that discipline comes from the Latin root *disciplinare*, which means to teach. To teach another human being requires that we have a working relationship with our disciple, or one who is open to being taught.

Shapiro and White have added a pioneering dimension to discipline, offering mindfulness as the foundation for a loving approach to parenting our children. *Mindful Discipline* helps us as parents cultivate the most important quality of parenting: the quality of mindful presence. In the face of uncertainty, vulnerability, and stormy emotions, nothing is more powerful than being fully here, fully embodied, fully present. Mindfulness, the art of being fully present, is the source of our most intuitive, wise, and attuned parenting.

This book offers fifteen mindful awareness practices that help us increase our capacity to be present, clear minded, and heartfelt as we set limits. These practices are something my own work at the Greater Good Science Center at the University of California, Berkeley—as well as loads of other academic research—has shown will help us raise emotionally intelligent, happy, and healthy children. And I've found that in addition to helping us become better parents, these practices also support our own development as individuals.

We don't have to be perfect parents or disciplinarians; as Shapiro and White write, "The times we lose our cool or act unskillfully create an opening where humility, forgiveness, and compassion can bring us closer with our child and grow each of us up in the process." But how do we find joy (and more skillful parenting) in our imperfect moments? Through the mindfulness practices detailed in this book! *Mindful Discipline* will help your whole family grow together.

> —Christine Carter, PhD
> Author, *Raising Happiness: Ten Simple Steps for More Joyful Kids and Happier Parents*

FOREWORD

by Dean Ornish, M.D.

I love this book. I wish it were packaged with every pregnancy test.

Often, we are presented with false choices. Is it fun for me or is it good for me? Well, why not both?

Should I be a tiger mom who strictly disciplines and represses my kids or a free spirit who coddles my child? Well, neither.

In *Mindful Discipline*, Drs. Shauna Shapiro and Chris White eloquently present a third, middle path—a relationship-centered approach that combines unconditional love *and* healthy boundaries and provides mentorship *and* space in a nurturing environment that allows for making mistakes as a pathway to wisdom.

This remarkable book weaves together ancient wisdom teachings with modern science to provide new perspectives on parenting, discipline, and what is needed to raise a healthy, emotionally intelligent, and joyful child.

Discipline can be limiting or liberating, depending on the intention and awareness behind it. When we consciously choose to limit what we're doing, it liberates us.

Discipline provides freedom if it's freely chosen because it enables us to do things and to express ourselves in ways that we otherwise might not be able to do. For example, musicians practicing scales may feel it's a little tedious at times, but the scales enable them to express themselves more freely by playing beautiful music.

For almost forty years, I have directed a series of clinical research studies proving that comprehensive lifestyle changes may reverse the progression of coronary heart disease, early-stage prostate cancer, type 2 diabetes, and other chronic diseases. These lifestyle changes include healthy nutrition; increasing exercise, yoga, and meditation; and having more love and social support.

More recently, we found that when you change your lifestyle, it changes hundreds of your genes—turning on good genes that keep us healthy, and turning off genes that promote a variety of chronic diseases—in only a few months. We also found that these lifestyle changes begin to lengthen telomeres, the ends of our chromosomes that control how long we live, thus beginning to reverse aging on a cellular level. All of these lifestyle changes are powerful, but it takes real discipline to put them into practice.

Over the years, I've learned that in addition to these intrinsic benefits of changing lifestyle, having the discipline to choose *not* to do something imbues action with deep meaning and purpose, making it sacred—that is, the most meaningful, and the most joyful.

If it's meaningful, it's sustainable. "I feel deprived because I can't eat this food" is not sustainable. "I'm choosing not to eat this food because what I gain is so much more than I give up" is sustainable.

That's what the most enlightened spiritual teachers have taught through the millennia: how to live a joyful life, right here and now.

Mindful Discipline offers a revolutionary perspective on parenting. It reframes our understanding of what discipline means, identifying the healthy dimensions that are essential to well-being—from learning self-regulation and impulse control as a child to making wise lifestyle choices as an adult.

The teachings that underlie each chapter are presented with an openhanded invitation for all parents to grow individually alongside their children, and to learn to trust both their own and their children's innate wisdom. The authors also share their personal journeys with parenting as illustrations of the principles they discuss and demonstrations of how the cultivation of loving, mindful discipline serves the entire family.

Our social connections, beginning with the relationship between parent and child, are fundamental to health and happiness. Study after study has shown that social support—a research euphemism for love and intimacy—is perhaps the most important determinant of our health and well-being. People who are lonely, depressed, and isolated are three to ten times more likely to get sick and die prematurely than those who have a strong sense of love and community.

How we raise our children is a primary determinant of their capacity for love and intimacy. Drs. Shapiro and White recognize that deeply loving, attuned, courageous, and compassionate parenting facilitates health, well-being, and the capacity for self-discipline in children.

This kind of parenting is optimally supported by the practice of mindfulness, or the development of moment-by-moment attention and presence. It is from this place of centeredness and emotional clarity that parents learn to make the "disciplined" choices that best facilitate fulfilling relationships with their children while promoting the child's healthy development. As parents, meditation can help us quiet down our minds to be able to hear the still, small voice within that speaks clearly but quietly. We learn to trust our inner wisdom to help guide and refine our parenting in every moment.

At the deepest level, it is this loving presence that underlies all health, from our children to our families to our world, and it is this loving presence from which calm and centered discipline emerges. *Mindful Discipline* shows us how.

—Dean Ornish, M.D.
Founder and President, Preventive Medicine Research
Institute Clinical Professor of Medicine, University of
California, San Francisco
Author, *The Spectrum: A Scientifically Proven Program to Feel Better, Live Longer, Lose Weight, and Gain Health*

ACKNOWLEDGMENTS

It is a pleasure to acknowledge the many people who have contributed directly and indirectly to the development of this book. I am deeply grateful to my teachers and colleagues, who continue to guide me. In particular I would like to thank teachers Tara Brach, Sylvia Boorstein, James Baraz, Eugene Cash, Jack Kornfield, Jon Kabat-Zinn, Dean Ornish, Daniel Siegel, Alan Wallace, and Shinzen Young. I am also profoundly grateful to the teachers at the Center for Mindfulness, Health Care and Society, who introduced me to mindfulness-based stress reduction (MBSR) with such love, integrity, and grace.

I offer gratitude for the wisdom of Frances Vaughn and Roger Walsh, whose teachings and guidance have been invaluable these past twenty years. I am also thankful to Meinir Davis and Polly Ely for their unwavering commitment to my growth as a mother.

And I am profoundly grateful for my sangha of mothers, fathers, friends, and practitioners who are committed to bringing greater consciousness and love into each moment of this lived experience. I especially want to thank Eden Davis, Juna Mustad, Monique Ferris, Ann Curtis, Sergio Lialin, Micah Christopher Hollingsworth Miller, Miranda McPherson, Donna Carroll, Kat Davis, Michael Hebb, Ingrid Sanders, Jamie Wheal, Cassandra Vieten, Hans Keeling, Amy Novesky, Kristin Kaye, Justine Prestwich, Katie Vasieck, Dana Davol-Muxen, Shauna Witt, Miriam Burke, Mark Coleman, Peter Bauman, Donna Simmons, Trudie London, Mark Coleman, Cathy and David Krinsky, and Pete and Ali Yiangou. I am especially grateful to my coauthor and dear friend, Christopher White, whose perseverance, dedication, and deep love for this work are an inspiration.

Finally, I am deeply grateful to my family for teaching me that no matter what, I am loved. I am grateful to my grandparents, Benedict and Nancy Freedman and Grand'Mere; to my parents, Deane and Johanna Shapiro; to my sister, Jena Huston, and brother, Joshua Shapiro; to my beautiful aunties, Nancy Wayne, Deborah Benedict, Sam Howland, and Diane Shapiro, and my loving uncles, Tom Shapiro, Ken Jackson, Michael Freedman, and Barry Wayne; to my dear cousins and nephews; and most especially to my son, Jackson Ki.

May all children, and all beings, know they are loved.

—Shauna

I would like to thank the many wise teachers I have had over the years. There are too many to name all, but a few in particular: Sara Hurley, Eugene Cash, Roseanne Anoni, Mayuri Onerheim, Vince Draddy, and Hameed Ali for their profound guidance through the Diamond Approach; Dr. Gordon Neufeld for his invaluable insights into attachment and the heart he brings to his work; Dr. Dan Siegel for bridging neuroscience, relationships, and the Mystery with such precision and delight. Thanks to Eric Scher for use of his lake house when I was writing large portions of this manuscript. A special thanks to the men I am blessed to sit with regularly: your love and wisdom have been invaluable to me.

I am especially appreciative of my friend and colleague Shauna Shapiro for giving me opportunities to develop my knowledge and craft over the years, and for her wise insights throughout the writing of this book: I am deeply touched by your generosity. Both Shauna and I would also like to thank the editors and staff at New Harbinger Publications for helping us birth this book.

Thank you to my parents, Rich and Betsy, for the perfect blend of love, limits, and mis-takes: all apparently necessary for me to become who I am. A deep bow of gratitude to my two beautiful boys, Kai and Bodhi, for breaking my heart open again and again, simply by being who and what you are. And to my wife, Kari, the love of my life: my rock. Without you and the boys, I would be a shell of a man. Thank you for all your love, patience, and support.

And lastly, a deep bow of gratitude to the great Mystery that has given me life and blessed me with a thousand ways to know myself and the world around me. You gifted me my family, and with them enormous humility and heart. For that, I am forever grateful.

—Chris

Part 1

A Discipline We Can Feel Proud Of

INTRODUCTION

Do not doubt your own basic goodness. In spite of all confusion and fear, you are born with a heart that knows what is just, loving, and beautiful.

—Jack Kornfield, *The Art of Forgiveness, Lovingkindness, and Peace*

Parenting may be the most profound and meaningful endeavor of our lives. We are pushed out of our comfort zone day after day, challenged and made uncomfortable in ways we never imagined. But most of us would do it all over again in a heartbeat; our children are worth every drop of our blood, sweat, and tears.

And yet, none of us want this job forever. We hope the joys of *being a parent* continue indefinitely, but the *work of parenting* is another story. Children can be incredibly difficult at times, refusing to cooperate with even the most basic of requests, like "Will you please hang up your coat?" or "Can you be more gentle with your baby brother?" We do our best to keep our cool, to understand their perspective and respect their autonomy, but it can be terribly frustrating.

In our conversations with parents, two main themes emerge again and again. First, parents tell us they want to create a harmonious home that flows smoothly and is restful. We all want our homes to be nurturing and intimate environments that bring out the best in each family member. Second, parents express the desire that their children grow up into mature individuals who can increasingly steer their own ship. We want them to feel a sense of commitment to their own lives and to the people around them, and we want to help them develop the skills necessary to act in responsible and respectful ways. We hope that through the development of healthy *self-discipline* they will become empowered to enjoy happy, meaningful, and authentic lives.

A key to creating harmony in the home and helping children thrive is the practice of discipline. Over the last fifty years, much has been written about parenting and discipline. Some "parent-centered" approaches are focused primarily on getting control over children, but not on the long-term goals of healthy self-discipline. Other parenting books—sometimes called "child-centered" approaches—are written in reaction to the more authoritarian and controlling methods. These approaches can leave parents with the impression that children are fragile and can't handle not getting their way—that they must always be pacified or coddled to prevent "trauma." This is a misunderstanding of how emotional intelligence and resilience actually develop. The research is clear that discipline, when it is healthy and balanced, plays an essential role in the raising of emotionally intelligent, self-disciplined children who thrive (Grolnick 2009). We felt that a new approach—a "relationship-centered" approach—needed to be articulated in order to empower you as a parent *and* to support your child in one day being able to guide her or his own life with wisdom and integrity.

The word "discipline" often evokes strong emotional reactions, particularly because it is often used synonymously with "punishment." However, the original meaning of *discipline* is "to teach." The Mindful Discipline approach offers a conscious path toward *teaching* our children to find their innate wisdom while simultaneously transforming our house into a more restful and harmonious home.

Creating a harmonious home and supporting self-discipline in our children requires that we as parents become more self-disciplined. With intentional practice, our own self-awareness, self-regulation, and self-discipline coevolve and mutually support these qualities in our children.

By seeing discipline as a loving container for optimal development, we parents and our children can grow and learn together. As author and teacher Frank Marrero says, "Discipline is the obligation of relationship" (personal communication, 2010). We learn the value of respect and cooperation by experiencing teamwork in the home. We see firsthand both how personal responsibility is empowering and how it helps create a safe and restful place where all family members can thrive. It is the relationship—the context of love and respect—that motivates us beyond our personal needs and impulses, and inspires the development of self-discipline.

Nature's Plan

Here's the good news: raising children is not all up to us! Nature is on our side. Self-discipline, emotional intelligence, and resilience are hardwired into human growth and development.

In a way, your child is like a plant. She starts out as a seed: full of potential, but undeveloped. If the seed receives the nourishment it needs, it will grow roots, push its way out of the ground, and develop through various phases: shoot, sapling, and, eventually, a full-grown tree that bears the fruit of maturity.

You, the parent, are like a gardener. Your role is to provide the nourishment needed in order for the plant to survive and thrive. If the plant's growth seems to be stalled, you try first to understand what form of nourishment might be missing. More water? Which nutrients? Protection from other invasive species? A gardener knows that she can't simply shout at the plant to make it grow faster. Nor will pushing and pulling it result in a tree's maturing and bearing fruit before its time (Neufeld and Maté 2004).

Nature unfolds in its own way and its own time. We play an important role in our child's development, but it is not all up to us. Our job is to read our children's needs, do our best to provide the nourishment, and be patient. We must trust ourselves, our children, and the developmental process.

The Parent's Role

Our role as parents is to support nature in growing our children up by providing certain forms of nourishment. The nourishment that children need to become self-disciplined falls into five categories of experience that we call the five essential elements of Mindful Discipline: 1) unconditional love, 2) space, 3) mentorship, 4) healthy boundaries, and 5) mistakes. On one hand, children need to know that they are perfect exactly as they are. When we love them unconditionally and give them space to be themselves, they retain a basic trust in the world and a sense of their inherent value as human beings. Feeling a degree of autonomy, they remain curious, engaged, and develop an increasing sense of responsibility over their lives.

However, children also need mentorship and healthy boundaries. These two elements communicate to children, "While it is true that you are perfect as you are, it is also true that you have a long way to go." Children have a lot to learn about the workings of the world we live in, and it requires a great deal of time, guidance, and practice to develop the skills that comprise healthy self-discipline. Mentorship and healthy boundaries help children develop impulse control, emotional intelligence, and the ability to adapt in the face of adversity.

Lastly and perhaps most surprisingly, our mis-takes can end up nourishing our children. We write "mis-takes" instead of "mistakes" to signify that these are "missed takes"—moments or occasions when we missed the mark and need to correct course. In this way, mis-takes can be seen as potentially beneficial and nourishing, rather than simply bad or wrong. When we recognize our misstep and move to reconnect and repair, both we and our children learn and grow. Relationships are a messy affair, and children learn from seeing their parents' authentic struggles with self-discipline. The times we lose our cool or act unskillfully create an opening where humility, forgiveness, and compassion can bring us closer with our child and grow each of us up in the process. The shadow aspects of ourselves often lead to the deepest of healing and intimacy. The lotus flower grows in the muddiest of swamps: as the common Buddhist saying goes, "No mud, no lotus."

In order to provide the nourishment our children need, we need to first ensure we embody the right relationship with them. Nature has intended for the parent-child relationship to be a *loving hierarchy* (Neufeld and Maté 2004). Dependent young children are born into our loving arms and we are responsible for protecting, caring for, and guiding them. To be clear, we are not talking about the pathological and destructive form of hierarchy where parents are not attuned to the needs of their children and use and abuse them out of their own self-centeredness. Such *dominance hierarchies* are what characterize an unhealthy *authoritarian* approach to discipline.

But the limbic brain of a young child instinctively looks for a loving authority to take the lead in caring for him. (The *limbic brain* is the group of brain regions we share with all social mammals that is responsible for functions like caretaking of offspring and social-emotional learning and functioning.) The *permissive* approach to parenting leaves children feeling unsafe. Children are not meant to be in charge of their parents. Nature did not intend for them to run our households. There are times to let them practice leading, and times for democratic decision making, but a loving hierarchy is the most healthy arrangement for your child's development. A loving hierarchy provides the structure and boundaries required for our children to feel safe: to know that someone more experienced is at the helm. If we balk at this responsibility, our children and our families will suffer. We'll talk more about authoritarian and permissive styles of parenting—as well as the more nourishing authoritative style—in chapter two.

How Mindful Discipline Will Help You Parent

Mindful Discipline is an intentional, yet flexible approach to raising children of all ages. Although this book has focused suggestions for children ages one to ten, the concepts can be applied to any stage of development. We have found it most effective to focus on principles, rather than merely trying to apply techniques not rooted in deeper understanding. So here we offer a theoretical model accompanied by specific practices designed to help children grow into healthy, emotionally intelligent, and self-disciplined individuals. The guiding premise is that our role as parents is to discern what nourishment is needed, moment by moment, and to provide the nourishment that nature needs to bloom our children into their full potential. We offer this book to support you in becoming the most trustworthy, flexible, and intuitive gardener-parent you can be.

Parenting approaches to discipline often attempt to train children through the consistent application of punishments and rewards. This works great for dogs and other animals, but as we'll discuss, when used on children, the downsides to their development and to your relationship greatly outweigh the upsides. A key aspect of the Mindful Discipline approach is a shift from focusing on *behaviors* to instead identifying and responding to the underlying *needs* of your child. Sometimes the need is space, sometimes it is a firm boundary. Attending to these needs is the provision of nourishment and supports your child's development into a joyful, autonomous, and responsible young adult.

Seeing clearly is the crucial first step to providing what is needed. That is why mindfulness is a key element of the approach found in this book. *Mindfulness* can be simply defined as "attending to the present moment with a kind, curious attitude." It helps us see clearly what is actually here in the present moment, and invites us to be fully present with our children, to attune to them and see them clearly in their full sovereignty and vulnerability. When we begin to regularly incline our attention to what is actually happening *now,* rather than acting and reacting on autopilot, we begin to see clearly what is the most skillful, nurturing response in any given moment. Being in touch with reality—and in touch with our hearts—we learn to find our way to the *appropriate response* that will serve our children and our families. Finding the appropriate response is the practice of an entire lifetime, and is not reducible to a formula or technique. To respond appropriately we have to be present. Thus, Mindful Discipline invites us to wholeheartedly meet our children, ourselves, and life, moment by moment.

In addition to helping you see reality more clearly, the mindfulness awareness practices (MAPs) we offer throughout the book will help your parenting become embodied rather than conceptual (Siegel 2007).

Children respond more to our state of consciousness than to our words. When we are present, grounded, and clear, our children listen. When we are angry and attacking, they shut down or act out more. MAPs can help us self-regulate when we find ourselves contracted, frustrated, furious, or stuck. Having a practice to go to when you are about to become dysregulated can save your family from cycles of guilt, shame, resentment, and more acting out.

The intention is to discipline ourselves before disciplining our children. We need to learn to regulate and care for ourselves before we can care for our children. We can look to the wisdom of our body as a model: the heart pumps blood to itself first before pumping blood to the rest of the body. If it didn't, the heart would die, and then the rest of the body would die. We as parents need to learn how to bring self-regulation and self-care to our own lives so that we can help cultivate these nourishing capacities in our children.

Finally, we want to acknowledge the challenge of writing a book for parents. We do not want this to be another book that talks to you from an ivory tower of what you *should* do, and we definitely do not want to add to any feelings of guilt. We know parenting is hard, because we *are* parents. For us personally, parenting has been the most challenging journey we have embarked upon, and we are right in the thick of it with you. We offer this book with humility and with the knowledge that chaos and challenge will be part of the process. Sometimes you will have the patience of a saint. Other times, you will be pushed beyond your edge. Please hold our suggestions as a set of best practices, knowing that we are right there with you, stumbling along and making plenty of messes ourselves.

We have found that what is most important is not to try to be perfect, but rather to allow space for the messes and imperfections, and to practice holding them in a context of self-compassion. Becoming aware of our parenting patterns and reactions can be quite painful, and it is essential to bring an open, nonjudgmental heart to as many moments as we can. When we hold our difficult feelings—even the seemingly unforgivable ones—with compassion, we set the stage for healing and growth. As parents, we must learn to trust ourselves. As Jack Kornfield reminds us, "Do not doubt your own basic goodness. In spite of all confusion and fear, you are born with a heart that knows what is just, loving, and beautiful" (2002, 9).

Our deepest desire as parents is to see our children thrive—to see them grow into healthy, joyful, emotionally intelligent beings. Our aspiration is to support them in this process. Pause for a moment and feel the wholesomeness and natural goodness of this intention. You care. You love your child. You can trust this. And yet, lived experience often becomes far removed from this natural and deeply wholesome love. We become lost in a wilderness of chaos and confusion and we are searching for our path back. Mindful Discipline is an approach to parenting that helps guide us effectively back toward this innate path of love and wisdom.

How This Book Is Organized

This book has three parts. In the first five chapters, we outline a new approach to discipline called Mindful Discipline. Mindful Discipline is an integrative approach that embraces discipline as one dimension of a healthy, wise, and loving relationship. We introduce mindfulness, a powerful practice that transforms how we see and experience our children. Mindfulness supports us in skillfully providing the most appropriate response to our particular child in his or her particular circumstances. Bringing mindfulness to discipline will transform the way in which you parent, and the way in which you live. We reframe the concept of "discipline" to help you see it with fresh eyes. This new understanding helps you make sense of the often opposing approaches to discipline currently espoused in our culture. From this reframed and cohesive big-picture view, we parents are able to recognize that children need a variety of experiences to grow up whole and reach their full potential: not just love and respect, not just autonomy and space, not just teaching and emotional coaching, and not just limits on their behavior.

In the second part of the book, we focus on the five essential elements of Mindful Discipline and how they lead to self-disciplined, emotionally intelligent, and resilient children. Each chapter from six to ten describes a core element—unconditional love, space, mentorship, healthy boundaries, and mis-takes—and what qualities develop when that element is provided. We offer practical examples of how to incorporate each element into everyday life, as well as specific practices to increase your embodiment of a loving authority. The final chapters describe how these five elements affect the wiring up of the brain in a healthy way, allowing our children to enjoy happy, meaningful, and fulfilling lives.

The end of the book contains resources to support you as you continue on this path of parenting. We offer appendices, a references section, and a list of suggested further readings.

At the deepest level, we as parents already know the principles detailed in this book. Our intention in writing *Mindful Discipline* is simply to help you draw upon your innate wisdom. This book is offered as a reminder that *the nourishment your child needs is already in your naturally wise and loving heart*. Life has decided that you are exactly who your child needs to reach her full potential. Yes, we as parents are far from perfect, but our love and commitment is deep. Trust yourself. Trust your child and his process. Enjoy the journey!

1.

WHY DISCIPLINE MATTERS

The Key to a Healthy Mind and a Fulfilling Life

Discipline leads to freedom.

—The Buddha

In part, the purpose of discipline is to help create harmony so that our homes and our family lives are nourishing and restful. And yet, there is another aspect of healthy discipline that often goes unnoticed.

What at first might seem paradoxical is the recognition that self-discipline and freedom go hand in hand. Freedom is the ability to know ourselves deeply, to bring a wise attention to each moment, and to be able to consciously respond to life instead of automatically reacting. Responding from a place of wisdom rather than fear liberates everything from relationships to career to ordinary moments at home with our family. Teaching our children self-discipline puts them on a path to freedom.

In this chapter, we define discipline and differentiate the two main uses of the word. We then share why the development of self-discipline is absolutely essential to living a rich, meaningful, and fulfilling life. The key question is: Can we create harmony in our home *and* support our child to become self-disciplined in a way that helps her remain healthy and open and develop her own authentic internal compass? The answer is a definite "yes."

What Is Discipline?

The word *discipline* is both a verb and a noun. In this book, we will refer to the verb form as *discipline* and the noun form as *self-discipline*. Both of these terms have healthy and unhealthy meanings, and it is the unhealthy meanings that cause many parents to reject the entire notion of discipline. We argue that it's time for parents to understand what *healthy* discipline is and how it supports healthy development for the entire family. By reclaiming discipline, parents stand poised to raise the bar for parenting in the twenty-first century.

The verb *to discipline* is often understood to mean "to intimidate" or "to punish," as in "I had to discipline my daughter today when she misbehaved." This exemplifies the *unhealthy* meaning of "discipline"—it describes principles and practices that are not effective at helping our children grow up healthy and become self-disciplined in the long run. Excessive use of fear, guilt, and shame as motivators will lead to a loss of vitality, emotional openness, and connection with your child. It also prevents her from developing the internal *desire* to be respectful and responsible and to do the "right" thing.

The healthy meaning of the verb form of discipline is "to teach"—which is something that can be done in a variety of ways that are supportive and that promote the development of increasingly empathic and ethical behavior in our child. The ways that we discipline our children—the ways we teach them—directly impact whether or not they develop healthy self-discipline.

The noun *self-discipline* can be defined as "control over one's own behavior." The unhealthy version is excessively tight control over one's behavior, with a loss of aliveness, flexibility, and heart. This unskillful version of behavioral control is rigid, rooted in fear, lacking in empathy and self-awareness, and not sustainable over time. It's akin to a broken pressure cooker—it periodically explodes in destructive ways.

So what does it mean to have healthy self-discipline? We define *healthy self-discipline* as "the ability to regulate one's own behavior and act in accord with one's values and aspirations." A self-disciplined child can control his impulse to shout out in class, and instead raise his hand. He can find ways to refrain from hitting his brother, and instead use words and nonviolent solutions to get his needs and desires met. Empathy and thoughtfulness are a natural part of healthy self-discipline.

This is what we ultimately want for our children, right? We want them to develop conscious control over their own behavior and act in a respectful and responsible manner. And we want them to do this out of their own desire and understanding instead of requiring external coercion or demands to become motivated. We want them to sense their impact on others and to use their own emotional intelligence as a guide. Our intention is that their self-discipline becomes sustainable and self-correcting.

Ready for the good news? Self-discipline is the natural outcome of healthy human development when all five essential elements of nourishment—*unconditional love, space, mentorship, healthy boundaries,* and *mis-takes*—are provided. And when you practice Mindful Discipline on a regular basis, you will begin to provide that nourishment for your child intuitively and with ease. These relational experiences affect the wiring up of your child's brain, the opening of his heart, and his developing capacity for self-discipline.

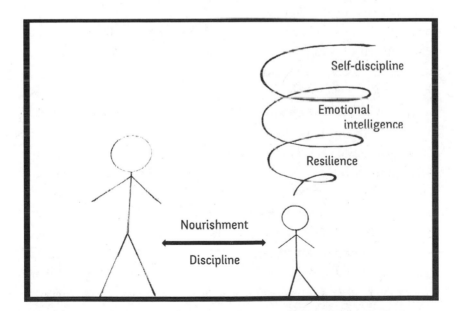

Figure 1: The Transmission of Discipline

The Value of Healthy Discipline

Healthy discipline in the home is important for four primary reasons.

1. Discipline creates harmony in the home.

2. Discipline supports mental health and a sense of well-being.

3. Discipline is needed for us to function optimally and reach our full potential.

4. Discipline ultimately leads to the resolution of behavioral problems.

Harmony in the Home

We all want our homes to be safe and nourishing places where we can be authentic and relaxed and share intimacy. We want the home to be a place of rest. When we regularly meet our children's needs—physical, relational, and maturational—they feel better, act out less, and become more capable of contributing to harmony in the home. Discipline starts with bringing our children to a state of *physiological rest* by meeting their needs. This is not rest strictly in the sense of non-activity. Rather, it's that a child is able to relax free of the constant pursuit of getting basic needs met. This allows him to shunt energy into other endeavors, such as learning to be a team player or problem solving on his own.

And because you meet his needs consistently, your child will remain deeply trusting of your guidance. Because you allow him a high degree of autonomy, he will not have the compulsion to act out in order to protect his sense of sovereignty. When it comes time for you to step in and set a clear boundary, he will be much more likely to listen and follow your guidance because he knows you are on his side. Your embodiment and communication of discipline helps organize the energetic and relational flow of the house into the greatest possible harmony and creates a feeling of *home* that is nourishing to the entire family.

Mental Health and Well-Being

Your child's overall health and experience of life depend on the development of her body and nervous system—and many factors go into that development. But the area of the brain that is perhaps most responsible for mental health and the experience of well-being is the middle regions of the prefrontal cortex (PFC). This area—often called the CEO of the brain—is responsible for a range of functions, from self-regulation to impulse control, capacity for attuned relationships, and self-insight and intuition (Siegel 2007; see appendix A for more details).

What Dr. Daniel Siegel found after years of reviewing the attachment and neuroscience research is that a secure attachment relationship leads to the child developing many of the same capacities that neuroscience attributes to a healthy middle PFC. (For more on attachment, see appendix B.) Simply put, when you attune to your child, and then meet her needs in a relatively consistent and reliable way, her PFC wires up and connects itself to other regions of her brain optimally. This process of *integration*—the connecting up of different parts of the brain into a coherent whole—is what underlies mental health and the development of self-discipline.

When her PFC wires up properly, your child develops the necessary tools to live a joyful and fulfilling life. With a healthy, integrated brain, she can handle life's ups and downs. She won't go into a tailspin every time she doesn't get her way or is not seen in the way that she had hoped to be seen. Your practice of Mindful Discipline, by strengthening the formation of her PFC, brings balance, resilience, and freedom to her life.

It also allows her to have deep and fulfilling relationships, which are a key ingredient to mental health and resilience. As she comes to know her inner world and the inner world of another person more intimately, she will experience greater connection and wholeness. Greater connection in turn will help her to move beyond her tendency for self-concern and to begin caring for other people, in keeping with the truth that everyone is precious and worthy of love and respect. As Marianne Williamson says, "Relationships are part of the vast plan for our enlightenment" (1992). We are encouraged to grow beyond our fearful selves for those we love. Love begets more love, and with each pass of the spiral, life becomes ever more fulfilling.

Optimal Functioning and Becoming Fully Ourselves

A disciplined mind and brain not only *feels* better, but *functions* better. Full brain development takes at least twenty-five years, and at every step of the way the PFC supports our functioning. A healthy, mature PFC is like a CEO in the boardroom. She has access to many different voices in the room—the managers, the human resource personnel, the lawyers, the accountants, the marketers—and each has its own area of expertise and set of priorities. The CEO listens to the different perspectives and then combines all of the information with her values and her vision for the future to make wise decisions for the company. If all goes well, the organization as a whole starts to move in harmony to implement the plan. The result is smooth functioning and productivity.

When fully developed, your PFC is highly integrated with many other regions of your brain that are designed for specific functions: regulating the body and the emotions, attuning to and communicating with others, thinking, planning, problem solving, and so on. Because it is connected to widespread regions such as the brain stem, the limbic system, and other areas of the cerebral cortex, your PFC can effectively receive signals and modulate the flow of energy and information throughout your brain. Like a CEO, it listens to the competing needs in any given situation, prioritizes the needs, and then takes action. To do so, it must downregulate the flow of energy through certain circuits and support flow through others. When the PFC is functioning optimally, the end result is a highly coordinated flow of behavior in alignment with your values and long-term intentions. You become able to live your life with self-descipline and integrity.

When we as parents become self-disciplined, it greatly benefits our children. For an example of how it works, say you are at a friend's house and your girls are out in the yard playing. You suddenly hear them both screaming and run out to see what is wrong. Your reactive, impulsive self says, "We have to save them!" But you arrive to find they are just playing, though both are still screaming like banshees. Your more judgmental self says, "They should not be screaming like that. It is inappropriate." And your impulse switches to wanting to scream at them for screaming. But instead of acting on these initial impulses and judgments, you take a breath and try to calm down before doing anything. Insights from your more thoughtful self include, "They are just children having a good time. I still want them to stop screaming. But I need to calm down first, before speaking. I was really scared." The resulting action: a deep breath, and then, "Hi girls, you having fun? Great. Can you tone it down just a bit? It's a little rough on our ears. Thank you."

This is how your capacity for integration—at the *intrapersonal* level as well as the *interpersonal* level—can lead to wise and compassionate action as a parent. Through processes of self-insight, self-regulation, impulse control, response flexibility, empathy, and attuned communication we can become capable of very high levels of functioning in all arenas of our lives. Remaining mindful and integrated are the keys to performing our best when it counts the most. These practices and abilities are the essence of self-discipline for us as adults, and they are the same capacities that we are trying to support in our children as they grow and mature.

In addition to optimal functioning in life and in relationships, we each have a drive within us to find out who we truly are: to live an authentic life that is in keeping with a deep and constant voice within us. We all want to find out who we are and what our gifts are, and to develop those gifts and share them with the world. But knowing who we are and what we love is only part of the story. It takes discipline to sit down and put in the ten thousand hours needed to really master our trades, especially on the days we don't feel like it (Gladwell 2008). And how about getting up on that stage when you are really frightened, or putting out that album or book not knowing how it will be received?

Becoming fully ourselves requires that we wrestle with our fear and sense of inadequacy, and yet continue to lean toward the very edge of what wants to be born through us. To live an authentic life and really give your gifts to this world requires a healthy balance of spontaneity and the development of self-discipline.

So yes, self-discipline means getting out of bed every morning and going to work. Yes, it means taking care of the basics like paying bills and buying butter. Yes, it means not fighting with every person with whom you disagree. But self-discipline is also essential for us to bloom into our unique fullness. And as parents, we value and practice self-discipline for the freedom it will impart to our children and their lives.

The Resolution of Behavioral Problems

One important role of parenting is guiding our children in taking responsibility for greater and greater portions of the "work" of daily life as they mature. We all hope that one day they will be able to brush their own teeth, get along with each other, and do their homework without our having to badger them. Their growing self-discipline supports our transition from constant enforcer and helps to resolve behavioral problems.

Once our children become better able to regulate their own emotions, control their own impulses, take responsibility for their actions, and treat others respectfully, our work as parents is significantly reduced. There is more time and space for us to enjoy and take delight in our children, instead of constantly monitoring and policing them. Sure, they will still act out and be irresponsible from time to time, but they will have the capacity—and more important, the *motivation*—to set things right on their own.

Once we have seen the benefits of a mindful approach to discipline, it becomes important to connect to our own specific values and long-term intentions for our children, so that we can raise our children with purpose and integrity. We invite you to take out a pen and a piece of paper and spend a few moments on the following exercise.

Exercise: Setting Our Compass

Ask yourself, "What are the ten to twenty qualities and capacities I hope my child ultimately develops?" Create a list that feels authentic and reflects what you hope for your child—not the list you think you *should* create.

This list will become your "North Star" when you are making discipline decisions in your home—what you look to to guide your decisions when you are feeling unsure of what to do. Share these aspirations with your partner or a friend. We have listed some of our own hopes in appendix C.

As important as it is to connect with our deepest desires for our children, it is equally important to hold these intentions lightly so that we don't squash the very thing we are trying to protect. The mindfulness awareness practice (MAP) for this chapter is one you can do to balance your heartfelt intentions for your child with a sense of wisdom and equanimity.

Mindfulness Awareness Practice 1:
Nonattachment

Sit comfortably with eyes closed and feel the stability and dignity of your body sitting here. Feel your connection with the ground underneath you. Feel how you are supported by the earth. Take a moment to connect with your body, releasing any obvious tension, and allowing the bones, the skeletal system, to hold you up, as you rest into a sense of being held, a sense of grounded ease.

Allow the breath to naturally flow in and out of the body. Feel the health and stability here in this moment. And as you're ready, call to mind the list of qualities and capacities you wrote down for your child in the preceding exercise. Feel the genuine goodness in your desires for your child, the beauty in each of your aspirations or intentions. Notice the embodied sense of each of the intentions. And then, with each one, gently let it go, resting back into the support of the breath, the body, and the earth.

For example, inwardly say, "joy." Feel the natural goodness and wholesomeness in you, which wants this for your child. What feelings emerge in your body and your heart? Take a couple of deep, slow breaths as you sense yourself. Then, when you are ready, let any attachment you have to this outcome gently float off.

This practice of nonattachment cultivates in us a sense of equanimity as we relate to "what is." This practice allows us to feel the beauty of our intentions, while also holding them lightly, not as an ultimate end, but as a general direction for the heart's compass. Setting the compass of our heart, we move forward, but in a relaxed way; we trust the intelligent unfolding of life.

Summary

The development of healthy self-discipline is essential if our children are to live happy, meaningful, and fulfilling lives. Our job as parents is to provide healthy discipline encounters informed by the five essential elements of Mindful Discipline—unconditional love, space, mentorship, healthy boundaries, and mis-takes—so our children will grow into emotionally intelligent, resilient, and self-disciplined adults. In doing so, we must draw on our own maturity in order to adequately support our children in becoming fully themselves. And what better opportunity than parenthood to continue maturing in order to express our love in the most nourishing ways possible? Through the relational practice of Mindful Discipline, we can transform the challenges of parenting into growth and wisdom.

> For one human being to love another...that is perhaps the most difficult task that has been entrusted to us... the work for which all other work is merely preparation. It is a high inducement for the individual to ripen...a great, demanding claim upon him, something that chooses him and calls him to vast distances.
>
> —Rainer Maria Rilke, *Letters to a Young Poet*

2.

HOW SELF-DISCIPLINE DEVELOPS

Growing From Impulses to Judgments to Authenticity

How much more precious is a little humanity than all
the rules in the world.

—Jean Piaget, *The Moral Judgment of the Child*

In the last chapter, we reframed discipline as a key ingredient to harmony
in the home and to a meaningful and fulfilling life for your child. In this
chapter we will go a little deeper into how discipline is a *transmission*
from parent to child that supports a natural *internal process*, ultimately
allowing the child to become a self-disciplined, emotionally intelligent,
and resilient adult.

Our children's ability to choose skillful responses instead of automatic,
fear-based reactions requires basic building blocks. Our task as parents is to
support these naturally developing building blocks so our children can
unfold into self-motivated, self-directed beings capable of responsible
actions and respectful interactions. When children grow up feeling pro-
tected and loved, seen and accepted for who they are, supported toward
increasing autonomy and competence, drawn toward empathy and

compassion, and taught how to adapt to circumstances beyond their control, they develop easefully and bear the fruit of maturity.

There are never any guarantees when it comes to raising children. Sometimes children who come from the worst home environments emerge as wonderful people. And at other times, people who have seemingly been provided love and caring attention end up selfish and undisciplined. And yet, certain environments and styles of discipline have a much greater chance of supporting children in growing toward health and maturity.

Common Approaches to Discipline

The three styles of parenting we described in the introduction are very different, but they share a common goal: they can be thought of as three different attempts to help children grow up. Each of these approaches—permissive, authoritarian, and authoritative—reflects different views of what children are and what they need to become self-disciplined (Grolnick 2009).

The *permissive* approach partakes of the belief that children are inherently good and do not need limits or guidance to become self-disciplined. The view is that the child simply needs love and respect and self-discipline will emerge in time.

This philosophy may feel right and consistent with your beliefs, but the research shows that more than love and respect alone is necessary to support the development of self-discipline. The research of Diana Baumrind and others has shown that children who grow up without healthy boundaries and age-appropriate behavioral expectations are more likely to be lacking in self-regulation, impulse control, achievement motivation, and cognitive and social abilities, and that they remain more self-centered and have higher rates of drug use than children of authoritarian or authoritative parents (Grolnick 2009).

The *authoritarian* approach is based on the belief that children are inherently bad and that they need to be manipulated into self-discipline to survive in a harsh and dangerous world. To do this, you punish children when they are bad and reward them when they are good.

The authoritarian approach may feel familiar to you, and may even appear sensible. But before using an authoritarian approach with our sons and daughters, there are a few questions we must ask ourselves:

- Do I want my children to experience life as mostly a threat?

- Do I want my children to only follow orders from some outside authority?

- Do I want them to respond to situations only through rigid application of "the rules"?

- Do I want my children to become cut off from their own internal guidance and emotional intelligence?

- Do I want my children to pay the mental and physical health costs associated with this more punitive and controlling approach?

Research on parenting outcomes amply shows that the authoritarian approach can obtain short-term compliance, but does not lead to healthy, sustainable self-discipline. So for the sake of your child's long-term growth and self-sufficiency—and for the sake of your relationship with him or her—we recommend limiting authoritarian moments wherever possible.

The *authoritative* approach views children as having the seeds of both good and bad behavior within them, and believes it is the parent's responsibility to nurture and invite the "good," while compassionately tempering the "bad." The authoritative style recognizes that both love and limits are necessary for a child to grow into a healthy, self-disciplined, emotionally intelligent, and resilient human being.

The authoritative style naturally supports the development of emotional intelligence. *Emotional intelligence* can be defined as "the ability to perceive and regulate emotion, and to act in personally and socially intelligent ways." Emotional intelligence is an innate developmental potential within human beings. It is not something that is downloaded, but rather it is a set of inherent capacities that we merely need to support (Neufeld and Maté 2004). When our children's natural propensity for emotional intelligence is supported, they grow up attuned to the inner world of people—both their own inner world and the desires, feelings, and perspectives of others as well. Through increasingly accurate perception of this rich interior landscape, our children become better able to regulate the flow of emotional energy and harness its power in service of what they value and aspire toward. Emotional intelligence is increasingly being recognized for its value in promoting a healthy, successful, and meaningful life (Goleman 1995).

Resilience is another quality that is supported by an authoritative style of parenting. *Resilience* can be defined as "the ability to persevere, adapt, and bounce back in the face of stress and adversity." When life bears down on our children, we want them to be increasingly able to handle the stress and find a way through. We desire that the challenges of life actually make our children stronger, wiser, and more confident. In this way, they will become more courageous about trying new things and following their dreams, knowing that they can handle the ups and downs of life and learn whatever lessons life has in store for them.

We believe it is imperative to help children develop their own inner authority and self-regulating mechanisms. The authoritative approach avoids the pitfalls of authoritarian parenting by supporting the child's own emotional intelligence and resilience to develop and eventually replace the need for external control and guidance. When we give our children space, they learn most of what they need to know by directly experiencing the impact of their actions. In this way, they will pay attention to the present moment before them, and be increasingly able to feel the nuances of human interactions and respond in ways that are attuned, empathic, and reflective of the truth of our interdependence. Through their own experience, they will develop a natural reservoir of resilience to rely on when faced with challenges. Mindful Discipline is an authoritative approach designed to support the developmental capacities needed for our children to be authentic and compassionate.

The Development of Self-Discipline

To understand how self-discipline develops, it helps to understand the two *modes* within which humans exist and the three *levels* we go through on the road to self-discipline.

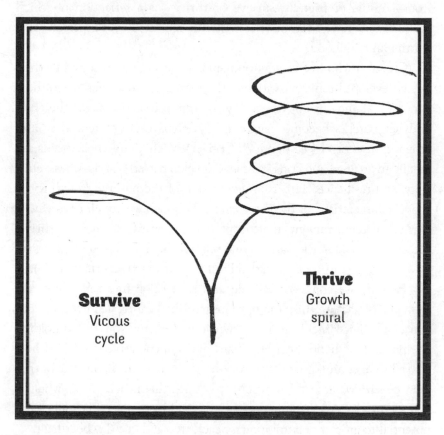

Figure 2: Two Modes: Survive and Thrive

A saying frequently attributed to Albert Einstein reflects these two modes: "The most important decision we make is whether we believe we live in a friendly or hostile universe." This points to the truth that the worldview we operate from affects everything from how we feel to how well we process information to how we behave. The *mode* we tend to live from—hostile or friendly, survive or thrive—is a reflection of which brain circuits have been most consistently recruited over a person's life, starting in childhood.

Children who live in environments consistently unattuned to their needs develop chronic activation of their stress circuits, even when there is not a real and current threat. Living from the *survive mode*, the child and her parents become caught in a vicious cycle of reactivity and attempts at control (see figure 2). Conversely, children whose needs are met in an attuned and consistent way develop patterns of openness, curiosity, and resilience. This is an expression of the natural growth spiral that is characteristic of the *thrive mode*. Although we are all born with a particular temperament that leans more toward survive or thrive, research shows that the parent-child relationship has profound effects on how we are predisposed to respond to life's stresses (Lieberman 1993).

How do we come to feel safe and to develop into self-disciplined individuals? Picture this: You have just finished eating a sweet and juicy peach. The juice is still running down your chin, and you are left holding the pit in your hand. Feel how hard and impenetrable it is? Feel how sharp its edges are? Why is this rock-hard pit there in the middle of that juicy peach? What is its purpose? If you open that peach pit up, what do you see inside? A soft, vulnerable seed. And in that seed lies all of the potential to grow into a full-grown peach tree and one day bear fruit.

Each child has such a pit within him. He has circuits in his brain and parts of his psyche that are devoted to one thing: survival. These parts of the brain have been with us from the time of our reptilian ancestors, and they generally operate through a portion of our autonomic nervous system (ANS) called the *sympathetic nervous system*. When these circuits are activated, we go into a self-protective mode of fight, flight, or freeze.

(The freeze reaction is actually mediated by an older branch of the para-sympathetic nervous system; see chapter 11 for more.)

This survival part of our psyche is healthy and natural. If we are to thrive we must first survive. The problem comes when these circuits become chronically activated. There are all kinds of physical and mental health costs when stress becomes chronic (Johnson et al. 2013). Approaches to discipline that rely on punishment, shame, and separation as ways to obtain compliance keep children in chronic states of stress. This style of discipline slows—and in some cases arrests—children's development because so much of their energy becomes focused on self-protection.

There is only so much energy to go around, and if the energy is chronically shunted to these survival circuits, then there is a paucity of energy going to the thrive circuits. The thrive circuits are predominately mediated by the *parasympathetic* branch of the ANS. If we meet our children's needs rather than resorting to punishment and manipulation, the energy shifts into the thrive mode, where health, healing, and growth predominate (Neufeld and Maté 2004). This is why using love rather than fear promotes healthy functioning and the development of self-discipline—those capacities are simply given the energy they need to develop.

When all goes well—when the child is satisfied and getting her needs met—the pit opens and the seed can begin to sprout. Energy shifts from survive to thrive, the seed pushes its roots down into the soil, and a shoot pushes up through the surface and begins to grow. With time and nourishment, the shoot becomes a young sapling, and eventually a mature tree that will flower and bear fruit.

This is the natural design, and our job as parents is simply to provide the nourishment. When the seed receives adequate nourishment it grows both roots of deeper *connection* and a shoot of further *individuation*. Eventually the tree will become strong enough that it does not need our constant tending, and we can simply sit back in the warm sun of summer and enjoy the delicious fruit of our labor.

Three Levels of Self-Discipline: The Impulsive Self, the Judge, the Authentic Self

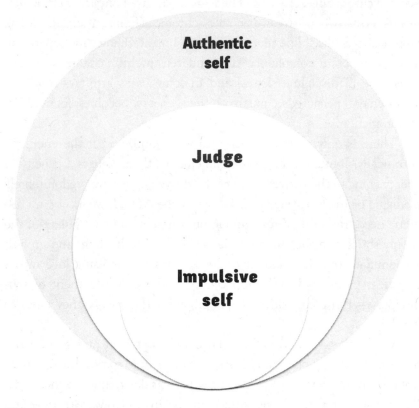

Figure 3: Three Levels of Self-Discipline

The plant metaphor is intended to help you visualize your child as part of a natural design that takes time to unfold. Our culture has conditioned us to believe that we are in control and are the ones who make everything happen—or, at least, that we ought to be. In this confusion we have come to treat our children as stones to be sculpted rather than plants to be nourished (Neufeld and Maté 2004).

When given the support they need to stay mostly in the thrive mode, children grow through three levels of self-discipline: the impulsive self, the judge, and the authentic self (see figure 3).

The Impulsive Self

Babies are all instinct and impulse. You as a parent are there to support their instincts when they are life-affirming and nourishing, and to intervene when they are not. You help them to feed when they are hungry, for instance, and help them get to sleep when needing rest. But you intervene and create boundaries when, for example, your nine-month-old starts to put a nickel in her mouth, or your toddler starts to run out into traffic. Nature has put young, impulsive creatures in the care of wiser adults for protection, care, and guidance.

Our instinctual brain is an important part of our wholeness, but its impulsiveness can get our children into trouble. As parents, we want to preserve the healthy instincts but rein in our children's dangerous behaviors, until they learn to tell the difference and can modulate their impulses themselves. The same is true for transgressions with other people: when our children are being disrespectful, we gently help them to behave in more appropriate ways. Close external parental guidance is necessary for young, impulsive children through at least the first seven years of life.

The Judge

The judge is a layer of the developing psyche that helps us behave independently of our parents and authority figures. It is largely composed of the ideas, beliefs, and judgments handed down by adults about what is good and bad, right and wrong. We study and memorize our parents' values and rules because we need to be on their good side to get our basic needs met. But the judge also gathers "rules to live by" simply from the child exploring his world and learning what works and what does not, what is dangerous and what is safe. The judge can be thought of as a rulebook in the mind, and its ultimate goal is to keep us safe.

It is like having a little parental voice inside your head that reminds you of the right thing to do when your impulsive self would have you grab that third cookie. This rulebook is a natural and normal development for human beings; it helps our children navigate the world on their own—to stay away from the hot stove without us having to remind them. It supports children by helping them to act in harmony with the cultural expectations of the people with whom they interact. When children succeed in doing the right thing, they feel proud and competent, and receive positive feedback from the world. So the judge is a healthy and necessary first step in that direction, but it is not the end game that nature intended.

There are two aspects of the judge that make it a less than wise and compassionate guide to respectful and responsible behavior. The first is that this internal rulebook does not carry true wisdom, but is rather a reflection of what has worked in the past. Applying old strategies that worked at home with mom and dad may not be what the current life situation calls for. In this way, the judge is more historical and reactive than present-focused and responsive. The second aspect of the judge that can be problematic is its tendency to treat us with harshness and intimidation rather than kindness and encouragement. Although it is trying to protect us and keep us safe, the *way* it does so can create internal feelings of shame, guilt, and fear. The judge often plays the role of the righteous ruler in our head, reprimanding us when we go off course.

The judge is not all bad; it does help us evaluate situations based on past knowledge. And yet, it is most helpful when used like training wheels to guide our child roughly between the ages of seven and fourteen; that is, until she begins to develop her own authentic value system and emotional intelligence. Once she develops her own internal compass, she can use her naturally wise and loving heart—her authentic self—to guide her toward respectful and responsible behavior based on the truth of *this* moment.

The Authentic Self

Beginning in adolescence, we can grow beyond both our impulsive self and our judges. Not all do so, but in our late teens, we can begin to mature into our *authentic self*. At this stage of self-discipline, we become acutely interested in what *we* feel, what *we* see, and what *we* believe about the world. We begin to close ourselves off somewhat to the influence of our parents and the rules and roles of society. It is a time of discovery, when we begin to find our own North Star and internal compass to guide us toward what we value and aspire to (Neufeld and Maté 2004).

As more time passes and we enter our twenties, we can become even more self-aware. We begin to track when impulses and judgments are arising in our minds and bodies and are trying to gain control over our behavior. We become more capable of not acting from our histories. We begin to discriminate our real-time insights, values, and vision for the future. From the authentic self, we can override our unconscious "go system" and instead consciously choose the best course of action from our more informed, better regulated "know system." This capacity— what we call *mindfulness*—is the heart of Mindful Discipline and the key to conscious parenting.

The capacity to be mindful, authentic, and empathic is a result of a well-developed middle prefrontal cortex, which greatly tempers the limbic system's reactivity. When we as parents consciously choose to become more mindful, the PFC grows like a muscle and supports our own self-discipline, emotional intelligence, and compassionate action (Siegel 2007). This in turn nourishes the PFCs of our children, supporting their well-being and the natural development of healthy self-discipline.

When choosing an approach to help our children develop self-discipline it is essential to consider the following:

1. How does the discipline affect our relationship?

2. How does it impact my child's authentic desire to be respectful and responsible?

3. How does it affect my child's emotional intelligence?

4. How does it impact my child's long-term development?

By choosing a style of discipline with these questions in mind, you can remain conscious of the natural tension between short-term compliance and the long-term effects of your attempts to teach your child and create harmony in the home.

Supporting the Development of Self-Discipline

Since discipline is a natural process that promotes greater integration and order in the brain, the question should be, How can I best support this process?

We can start by aiming to at least do no harm. When we manipulate our children regularly or frequently scare them into compliance, we can end up creating unhealthy levels of fear and anxiety that lead to more disintegrated patterns of neural firing and wiring. Sure, we will make mistakes. But if we trust that maturation does naturally lead to emotional intelligence and self-discipline, we will be less likely to over-interfere and disrupt this natural developmental process that culminates in our child growing into her authentic self.

We can further support our children in becoming self-disciplined by holding the view that discipline is partly a transmission that flows from teacher to disciple; in this way, our embodiment and example become essential. The ways we interact with our children teach them how to develop control over their behavior. It is not simply a matter of teaching them the letter of the law; in fact *how* we teach (by example) is much more important than *what* we teach (the explicit rules).

The transmission of one's *way of being* is not some magical process that flows from one person to another through the ether (though it is quite magical). This process is firmly grounded in the actual structuring of the brain, both in the moment and over time: when the nourishment is provided, the PFC wires up in an optimal way conferring emotional intelligence and resilience to our child's skill set. If we relax into our own wise heart and simply allow the five essential elements to flow from our being intuitively, then we help our children to relax into their own innate wisdom.

Of course the questions arise: How do I, as a parent, embody this way of being with my child? How can I more consistently *be* what I want him to *become*? The concept of allowing our own wise hearts to guide our parenting may be simple, but it is by no means easy: we are complex and fallible people ourselves, and we also need support to embody our best intentions. This is why mindfulness is a foundational part of this book and this approach to discipline. Mindfulness is both part of our innate human capacity, and it can be stabilized and cultivated through disciplined practice. It is the state from which we can more consistently match our good intentions with our actions.

A mindful parent meets the present moment and her child with an open, interested, attuned, and discerning presence. Mindfulness allows us to see the present moment clearly, and thus respond in a skillful way, instead of automatically reacting impulsively or from the habitual patterns and conditioning stored in our judge. The more we practice this way of being, the stronger it becomes in us. The stronger it becomes, the more others—especially our children—feel it, learn from it, and become more integrated themselves. Mindfulness has the ability to transform both parent and child.

In the next two chapters, we will begin our exploration of the powerful practice of mindfulness and outline the Mindful Discipline approach. Before you go on to further chapters, take a moment to read and experience the following mindfulness awareness practice. In this practice we aim to embody the best parts of ourselves—the qualities that our closest friends and family love in us.

Mindfulness Awareness Practice 2: Being Who We Truly Are

Call to mind someone who deeply loves and respects you. Imagine what kind words they might say about you. Take these acknowledgments into your being. You may notice some doubt or discomfort arising, or you may not be able to think of anything. If this is the case, simply call to mind one or two good qualities—if nothing else, you can reflect on your own pure intention to become the best parent you can be for your child. Feel the goodness in your deep desire to love and care for your child.

Whatever qualities you call to mind about yourself, spend a few moments receiving and taking in the good and allowing the patterns of goodness, the qualities of goodness that naturally exist in you, to become stronger, clearer, and brighter. Then spend a few moments resting in this space. Finally, when you are ready, thank yourself for taking this time to affirm and strengthen these wholesome qualities and to rest in who you truly are. You may perhaps form an intention to bring these qualities with you as you move back into your daily life.

Summary

Discipline is ultimately a process of integration and health that is transmitted from brain to brain. When this transmission is joined with the innate developmental impulses and structuring processes within each child, the result is a self-motivated, self-directed being who is capable and wants to be respectful and responsible. Research shows us that both authoritarian and permissive styles of parenting do not routinely lead to healthy self-discipline. Rather it is an authoritative style that nourishes children through both love and limits, leading to healthy brain development that culminates in sustainable and emotionally intelligent self-discipline.

Each moment as parents, we face the age-old struggle between fear and love. Will we collapse into our judge and our reactivity, or will we trust our authentic selves to guide our families? Deep inside every parent's heart lies the wisdom and compassion needed to nourish our children. The opening line from many Buddhist texts reminds us of the wisdom and goodness inherent in each of us: "Oh nobly born, do not forget who you really are." Reminding ourselves of our own good hearts and our pure intentions supports us in being the best parent we can be.

3.

MINDFULNESS

Nourishment for Life and Parenting

The most precious gift we can offer others is our presence. When mindfulness embraces those we love, they will bloom like flowers.

—Thich Nhat Hanh, *Living Buddha, Living Christ*

Not long ago, I (Shauna) had been traveling, and was away from my five-year-old son Jackson for a week. I was finally home, united with my little one. I missed him dearly and wanted to reconnect, to let him know that I was home, present, and loving him. It was a beautiful Saturday morning, and I decided we would spend a day together at Muir Beach, a place we both love. I proceeded to pack up towels, beach toys, a picnic lunch, a change of clothes, sunscreen, water, and games. I shifted into doing mode and became carried away in the speed of the agenda. Jackson was in a much slower pace, and it took quite a while to get him dressed and out the door. However, finally, we were off, and we were going to connect and have fun (damn it).

As we walked through our front yard, Jackson paused to look at a trail of ants. "Come on, sweetheart, it's time to go to the beach," I said, calmly, but with a hint of agenda in my voice. However, he was already completely absorbed by the ants and without glancing up said, "Mom, come over here—look!" I could feel the growing agitation and contraction in my body. I paused a moment, noticing these uncomfortable sensations. Luckily, I had just returned from a week of teaching mindfulness, so some of the lessons were still fresh in my being. As I scanned my body, I breathed, and reflected: "What is my intention?" "Oh yeah, I want to have quality time with my son, let him know that I am here now and that I missed him." This wasn't a school day; we didn't actually need to be anywhere at a specific time. Could I simply relax my agenda and remember what it was that was truly important—Jackson, here, now, in this moment, wanting to show me the ants?

He continued to stare at the ants. I walked over to where he was squatting, sat down in the sunshine, and began to watch. He scooted closer and leaned into me. The sun was warm on my back. A tear came to my eye as I felt the poignancy and preciousness of the moment. This was the connection I was wanting all along: my little boy, resting against my body; both of us sharing the fullness of the moment together.

What Is Mindfulness?

Mindfulness is often referred to as a consciousness discipline. It is a way of training the mind, heart, and body to be fully present with life. Although often associated with meditation, mindfulness is much more than a meditation technique. It is a way of being, a way of living. Mindfulness is about presence—being here, now, completely. This capacity to be fully alive and fully awake is at the heart of being human—and at the heart of being a parent. A mindful parent is one who is committed to practicing being present and awake, and to listening deeply to her child, moment by moment.

Mindfulness depends upon awareness. A common way to understand what awareness is is to practice an awareness of the breath. Are you breathing right now? How do you know you are breathing? Your knowing can be an intellectual and conceptual knowing, but it can also be a felt sense; a knowing with your whole being. This deep knowing is mindfulness. Try it now: As you breathe in, know with your whole being, "breathing in." As you breathe out, know with your whole being, "breathing out."

Another aspect of mindful awareness is noticing without reacting. Notice, for example, the state of your mind right now. Is it clear and interested? Is it dull and fatigued? Is it concentrated? Knowing the state of your mind in this moment, without judging it, evaluating it, or trying to change it, is mindfulness. Now notice your emotional state—is there joy, sadness, fear? This noticing is mindful awareness of what is true, right here, right now.

Mindfulness is fundamentally a way of being; a way of inhabiting our bodies, our minds, and our moment-by-moment experience with openness and receptivity. It is a deep awareness; a knowing and experiencing of life as it arises and passes away in each moment. This awareness involves freedom from grasping on to what is occuring or from wanting what is occuring to be different. It simply knows and accepts what is here, now; for example, "My son just knocked over my tea and I am frustrated." I notice what is and create space for what is happening and my response to it. In this way, I become able to see clearly what's happening both inside and outside myself, and to respond with skill rather than simply reacting.

Mindfulness depends on our ability to see clearly, because how we perceive and frame this moment generates our reality, and in turn impacts how we respond. And in the example of my son and the tea, mindful awareness allows me to see not only the facts—that he spilled the tea and that I feel frustrated—but also his emotional state: "He did not knock it over on purpose, but because he's really excited right now."

When we are able to see clearly we move closer and closer to our authentic center, where we know what is the most skillful response in each moment. With my son and the tea, I can simultaneously perceive my own feelings and their roots, my impulses, my understanding of his development and state of mind, and my desire to parent him skillfully, and these all inform my choice of how to respond: "I am frustrated at having to clean up another spill. I want to yell at him right now. I also know he is only four and still learning to regulate and control his body. I will focus on regulating myself first, and then we will talk about what happened." Seeing clearly, I become more compassionate with myself and with him, and become able to parent him with love and authority.

Mindfulness is one of our most helpful companions when we feel overwhelmed and confused, and the way forward becomes lost. Later, there will be time to reflect on the parenting advice and techniques we find in books or from other parents, but in the heat of the moment we must find our own center and moral compass. As Jon and Myla Kabat-Zinn remind us, "Ultimately, mindful parenting is about seeing our children clearly and listening to and trusting our own hearts" (1997, 30).

Parenting is a calling: a place where we can be drawn through the power of love to continue stretching and growing as people. It is not unlike an extended meditation retreat where our children are the Zen masters brought in to push our buttons at every turn (Kabat-Zinn and Kabat-Zinn 1997). It is totally overwhelming in moments, but it is at the edge of our overwhelm that we learn to become more free and loving than we ever thought possible.

When we practice mindfulness, it supports us in remembering who we truly are: that we are more than our reactivity and our ingrained habits of relating. We begin to wake up to our authentic center of knowing and to focus on what is most important. We intentionally choose to be awake to this moment and to see clearly, with curiosity and compassion. This way of being begins to shift our brain circuits toward empathy, understanding, and a felt sense of our own wisdom. It supports our wise and loving parenting choices, and fosters wisdom and resilience in our children.

Three Core Elements of Mindfulness

Mindfulness comprises three core elements: intention, attention, and attitude. *Intention* involves knowing *why* we are doing what we are doing: our ultimate aim, our vision, our aspiration. *Attention* involves attending fully to the present moment instead of being pulled into the past or future. *Attitude,* or *how* we pay attention, enables us to stay open, kind, and curious. These three elements are not separate—they are interwoven, each informing and feeding back into the others. Mindfulness *is* this moment-to-moment process.

Intention

The first core component of mindfulness is *intention*. Intention is simply knowing why we are doing what we are doing. When we have discerned our intentions and are able to connect with them, our intentions help motivate us, reminding us of what is truly important.

Discerning our intention involves inquiring into our deepest hopes, desires, and aspirations. In chapter one, we asked you to make a list of the qualities and capacities you hope your children develop. Reflect on this list now and ask yourself, "Is this truly *my* list? Or are these qualities society has told me are important, rather than qualities I authentically hope for for my child?" This reflection can help you with the important work of teasing out your unconscious beliefs about what a good or happy person is from your more consciously chosen values and aspirations for your life and for your children. Listen deeply for the answers, allowing them to arise organically. This deep listening, with trust in the process and the timing, allows your truth to emerge at its own pace. Mindful attention to our own intentions helps us begin to bring unconscious values to awareness and decide whether those values are really the ones we want to pursue.

Intention, in the context of mindfulness, is not the same as (and does not include) striving or grasping for certain outcomes for our children or ourselves. Rather, as meditation teacher and psychotherapist Jack Kornfield puts it, "Intention is a direction not a destination" (personal communication, 2012). We step readily in the direction our intention points, but we step lightly, with open eyes, ears, and heart as well as the consciousness that life has its own say in the matter (whatever the matter may be) and that there is much we have yet to learn.

Attention

The second fundamental component of mindfulness is *attention*. Remember, mindfulness is about seeing clearly, and if we want to see clearly, we must be able to pay attention to what is here, now, in this present moment. Paying attention involves observing and experiencing our moment-to-moment experience. What is interesting is that as you begin to pay attention, you realize how much of the time you are tuned out, spaced out, not present. For example, how many times have you read a sentence over again because you really didn't take in the meaning the first time? Or driven somewhere only to arrive without remembering anything about the drive? The human mind is often referred to as a "monkey mind," swinging from thought to thought as a monkey swings from limb to limb. Mindfulness is a tool that helps us tame and train our mind so that our attention becomes stable and focused, and attention is the component of mindfulness that allows this focus.

Often, as we try to pay attention, our attention becomes tense and contracted. This is because we mistakenly think we have to be stressed or vigilant to focus our attention in a rigorous way. However, the meditation traditions teach us of a different kind of attention, a "relaxed alertness" that involves clarity and precision without stress or vigilance (Wallace 2006). This relaxed alertness is the kind of attention that is essential to mindfulness. Mindful attention is also deep and penetrating; as Bhiku Bodhi notes, "[W]hereas a mind without mindfulness 'floats' on the surface of its object the way a gourd floats on water, mindfulness sinks into its object the way a stone placed on the surface of water sinks to the bottom" (Wallace 2006, 7).

Attitude

Attitude, the third core component of mindfulness, comes into play once we have learned to intentionally pay attention in the present moment. When we do so, we may notice something: our mind is constantly judging. The attitude with which we pay attention is essential to mindfulness. For example, attention can have a cold, critical quality, or an openhearted, compassionate quality. The latter is what brings out the best of our humanity and our parenting, and it is what we are talking about when we speak in terms of mindfulness.

Attending without bringing the attitudinal qualities of curiosity, openness, acceptance, and love (COAL; Siegel 2007) into the practice may result in an attention that is condemning or shaming of inner (or outer) experience—yours or your child's. This may well have consequences contrary to the intentions of the practice; for example, we may end up cultivating patterns of criticism and striving instead of equanimity and acceptance.

These attitudes of mindfulness do not alter our experience but simply contain it. For example, if while we are practicing mindfulness impatience arises, we note the impatience with acceptance and kindness. We don't try to substitute these qualities for the impatience, or use them to make the impatience disappear. The attitudes are not an attempt to make things be a certain way, but an attempt to relate to whatever *is* in a certain way. By intentionally bringing the attitudes of COAL, we relinquish the habit of striving for pleasant experiences, or of pushing aversive experiences away. Instead, we attend to whatever is here. Doing so within a context of curiosity, openness, acceptance, and love not only makes it much easier to stay present, it can also transform our parenting.

Note that while mindfulness allows and accepts whatever is present, it also discerns between wholesome and unwholesome. For example, through the lens of mindfulness you can see that your daughter is throwing sand at her friend and causing harm. You accept that this is what is happening, and also notice your emotional response (anger, frustration, embarrassment). You regulate your emotions and make a skillful choice to firmly remove your daughter from the situation, without removing your love or harming your relationship with her or yourself.

It may be useful to you to think of mindfulness as a presence of heart as well as mind. In fact the Japanese kanji for mindfulness is composed of two symbols, the top meaning presence and the bottom translated as "heart" or "mind." Mindfulness involves bringing heartfulness to each moment—bringing our full aliveness and care to all of our experiences. This enriches not only our own lives, but the lives of our children as well.

The Role of Mindfulness in Parenting

Mindfulness is the foundation of conscious parenting and the Mindful Discipline approach. The three elements of mindfulness—intention, attention, and attitude—provide the soil from which wise and compassionate parenting can grow. As mindful parents we reflect deeply on our *intentions*: What is most important? What are our most heartfelt desires for our children and our family? We bring our full *attention* into the present moment so we can see our children and ourselves more clearly. We attend with an *attitude* filled with openheartedness, curiosity, acceptance, and compassion. Through this process of intentionally attending with kindness and care, mindfulness allows us to see clearly what is needed, and gives us the tools to meet each moment with acceptance and love.

Mindfulness serves as a foundation for each of the core components of the Mindful Discipline approach. For example, mindfulness invites a compassionate, nonjudgmental presence that helps our children feel safe, accepted, and loved simply as they are. Mindfulness supports a curious and inquiring attention, which leads to greater understanding and empathy for your child. Mindfulness helps us stay grounded and calm, and helps us regulate our own emotions. This creates an embodied presence that has a direct calming effect on our child's brain and nervous system, and models for them how to regulate their emotions in a healthy way. Out of this place of clarity and calm, both we and our children can make more skillful choices.

Finally, mindfulness allows us to recover more gracefully from our missteps and increases the likelihood of opening to a state of forgiveness and compassion. Parenting is a wild and bumpy ride filled with what our judge would call "mistakes." Without an intention to be mindful, we can become entangled in unconscious guilt, shame, and frustration, acting out of these without even knowing why. As parents, we need more care and compassion than we will at perhaps any other point in our lives. And although we hope that our partners, family, and friends will help us in this regard, we must begin to hold ourselves with the same kindness, compassion, and understanding we want to provide for our children.

Our own parents, teachers, relationships, and society have influenced us in ways known and unknown; our patterns have often become so ingrained that we do not realize we are engaging in them. We tend to live on automatic pilot, being pushed and pulled by our patterns, not fully awake and alive and free to the reality of the present moment.

Mindfulness counteracts this conditioning, training our mind in the ability to be with and *know* our experience as it arises and passes.

This requires sustained practice: the intentional training of our mind to pay attention in a caring, discerning way. This training is done through formal mindfulness meditation practice as well as informal mindfulness practices. The training begins here, now, in this very moment, because right now *is* the we can practice. Even this sentence can be read with mindfulness—feeling your body, your breath; perhaps recalling your intention for reading this book. Allow your intention to inspire and motivate you to practice in this moment; and now, in this one…

Cultivating Mindfulness

What we practice becomes stronger. When we practice mindfulness, we strengthen our capacity to be present moment by moment in a curious, accepting, and loving way. Mindful practice can be categorized into *formal* and *informal* practice; each kind of practice supports the other. The formal practice will support the ability to practice mindfulness "on the fly" in real life, and informal practice is meant to generalize to everyday life what is learned during the formal practice.

Formal practices, like sitting meditation, are geared toward cultivating mindfulness skills in focused and systematic ways. These can involve relatively brief daily meditation woven into one's day, or intensive days- or weeks-long retreats involving many hours of formal sitting and walking meditation based on centuries-old traditions. Informal practice involves intentionally bringing an open, accepting, and discerning attention to whatever we are engaged in—for example, reading, driving, eating, or parenting.

In this section, we provide two mindfulness awareness practices to help you get started. If you don't yet have a formal mindfulness or meditation practice, we invite you to begin with five minutes of formal meditation practice each day, using the Formal Mindfulness Exercise. If you do not have experience generalizing mindfulness principles to ordinary daily experience, we invite you to try the Informal Mindfulness Exercise the next time you do the dishes.

Before we begin, we offer instructions from my (Shauna's) father, who taught me to meditate when I was five years old. He said, "Imagine yourself sitting under a busy highway, and there are cars racing overhead. These cars are your thoughts. You notice the cars, but don't climb in and drive away. Notice the thoughts, but don't follow them. Instead, simply come back to the breath."

Mindfulness Awareness Practice 3:
Formal Mindfulness Exercise

Find a comfortable seated posture and rest here with the breath, feeling the natural flow of breath moving into the body and out of the body. There is no need to change or control the breath, simply feel it. And notice the quality of your attention as you attend to the breath. Can you infuse it with the attitudes of COAL—curiosity, openness, acceptance, and love? Whenever some other phenomenon arises in the field of awareness, note it, and then gently bring the mind back to the breathing. If any reactions occur, such as enjoying what arose in your mind or feeling irritated by it, simply note the enjoyment or irritation with kind interest, and then return to the experience of breathing. Each time you notice your mind has wandered off is a moment of mindfulness; the moment you notice *is* a moment of presence, so try celebrating the fact that you are back instead of judging yourself for wandering off. The mind wanders off a thousand times; we bring it back with our kind attention a thousand and one times, cultivating presence, trusting the process.

Mindfulness Awareness Practice 4:
Informal Mindfulness Exercise

Start by making a conscious intention to wash the dishes—just this once—as an informal practice in mindfulness, intentionally attending to all of your experience with curiosity, openness, acceptance, and love as you perform the task. Feel the soap and water on your hands, the weight of the plate you're holding; hear the sounds as the water splashes about. How does your body feel—your feet, your back, your arms? Are you present in this moment? How does your mind feel? What emotions and thoughts do you notice? Simply note what you find with interest and kindness. If your mind wanders off, you can simply connect to your breath, softly noting each inhale with "in" and each exhale with "out." Let your contact with the breath anchor you to the felt sense of the present moment. Now open your awareness into a relaxed, receptive state; opening to all experience that is here, now. By washing dishes in this way, or engaging in any activity in this way, you are actually training the mind and body in mindfulness, strengthening your capacity to be present for yourself, for your children, and for life.

We invite you to aim for ten to fifteen minutes a day of total practice. This book offers fifteen different mindful awareness practices for you to try. Choose the ones that feel most relevant and supportive to your current life situation. Be intentional, yet gentle with yourself. This kind of practice is not about being perfect, but more like riding a wave: there will be times you are carried along by the wave and times you fall into the ocean. No problem either way; both experiences have much to teach us.

Summary

Mindfulness is at the core of authoritative parenting, and is the foundation of Mindful Discipline. Mindfulness helps us discipline our children with authority, consistency, love, and skill, helping us see clearly where guidance, limit setting, and boundaries are appropriate, and where a softer, more expansive intervention is needed. Mindfulness gives parents the skill to see what is most appropriate and compassionate in any given moment. It helps us 1) clarify our values and intentions; 2) strengthen our capacity to be present; 3) increase our capacity for attunement and empathy; 4) increase our capacity for self-awareness, self-care, and self-regulation; and 5) increase our ability to accept what is happening and to appropriately respond.

Mindfulness connects us with our deep desire for our children to feel safe, loved, and valued, and to become emotionally intelligent, self-disciplined beings who thrive. We hold this intention for our children in our hearts; mindfulness helps us bring it to the surface so that it guides us moment by moment. Mindfulness does not give us all the answers, but allows us to better hear the questions.

Have patience with everything unresolved in your heart and try to love the questions themselves as if they were locked rooms or books written in a very foreign language. [T]he point is to live everything. Live the questions now. Perhaps then, someday far in the future, you will gradually, without even noticing it, live your way into the answer.

—Rainer Maria Rilke, *Letters to a Young Poet*

4.

THE MINDFUL DISCIPLINE APPROACH

Transmitting Self-Discipline

A wise mother knows: It is her state of consciousness that matters. Her gentleness and clarity command respect. Her love creates security.

—Vimala McClure, *The Tao of Motherhood*

The Mindful Discipline approach is holistic, flexible, pragmatic, and most importantly, focused more on *long-term development* than *short-term compliance*. Again, we are not talking about discipline as punishment, but as a constructive means of helping our children mature. The five essential elements of Mindful Discipline—unconditional love, space, mentorship, healthy boundaries, and mis-takes—are most naturally provided when we as parents are in a relaxed, grounded, and centered place. Our focus in presenting this approach is to restore you to your natural intuitions and sense of authority. We are not going to give you "the ten steps to perfect parenting" or say, "when your child does x, just do y and the result will be z." Parenting doesn't work that way—no relationship does. Instead, we want to equip you to see deeper than behavior, keep your cool in tough times, and mindfully take the reins and find your own way.

At the same time, we want to make this truth clear: *you are not ultimately in charge; life is.* It may sound contradictory when we say, "You must take the lead in caring for and guiding your children," and then turn around and say, "You are not ultimately in charge." But both are true. As parents, we are definitely responsible for doing the best we can to lead our children and our families in the direction of happy and fulfilling lives. We must lead our families with integrity. But at the same time we must remain humble and open to the dynamic and intelligent unfolding of life. In some ways, we are meant to be overwhelmed by this experience to the point that we regain our humility and perspective. Nothing builds greater trust within the human psyche than to be pushed beyond our ego's capacity to control everything, and have it still work out in the end. As songwriter Craig Minowa says, "Everything you need is here. And everything you fear is here. And it's holding you up. It just keeps holding you up" (2008).

Mindful Discipline Perspectives

Let's start with a big-picture perspective of Mindful Discipline—call it the view from 10,000 feet. It is this: the best way to help our children grow into their full potential is to take the attitude that we are growing up *together*. We have as much to learn as they do. With this attitude, we focus first and foremost on enjoying our children in our brief time together, and we aim to arrange our lives in a way that will best support our collective happiness and growth. We proudly assume our natural position in the order of things. We are not the creators or sources of our children's gifts and developing capacities. We are the gardeners supporting the dynamic intelligence of life. We aim to provide the nourishment that life needs to do its work. We recognize that life has chosen us to be this child's parent: for our gifts as well as our shortcomings. As much as possible, we try to relax, knowing that even in our missteps and confusion, things are unfolding as they should.

And finally, if on a given day we have some extra energy and focus, we practice mindfulness. We bring a mindful attention to the moment and circulate our breath and our awareness in a way that increases the shine of love through our bodies. We practice not in order to *get* something, but to *give*. We practice not in order to improve ourselves, but rather to become more fully who and what we are.

Moving in a little closer—to the view from 100 feet—we focus on principles, the pearls we can come back to again and again when we feel lost. The parent practicing Mindful Discipline focuses more on her children's long-term development of self-discipline, emotional intelligence, and resilience than on their short-term compliance. She is guided by her understanding of the unique needs of each of her children. She knows that applying parenting techniques without a deeper understanding will likely fall short, and may actually make things worse.

She knows that relationships are a dance and a journey, not a straight line. She knows that love comes in different flavors, and that each flavor nourishes different parts of the human psyche. She is intentional, yet flexible and pragmatic. She recognizes that parenting styles are actually best thought of in terms of parenting *moments*: that each situation has its own specific needs not prescribed by any dogma. She trusts her awareness and intuition when with her children, and actively learns and reflects on her parenting challenges when she has the time and space away from them. She recognizes that different people in her child's life will bring different qualities and have different shortcomings, yet also unique gifts to share. She trusts others in her village to help raise her child.

And most importantly of all, the mindful parent teaches discipline primarily by embodying it. Whether it is by handling stressful situations with confidence and grace, or by falling apart and modeling ways to recover, she teaches her child primarily through her own way of being with her family and with the world. She trusts the ups and downs of life, the developmental process, and the power of presence.

The Key Principles of Mindful Discipline

- Focus on long-term development more than short-term compliance.

- Be intentional, yet flexible and pragmatic.

- Understand principles rather than memorize techniques.

- Use the models *away* from your child; trust your intuitions when *with* her.

- Model discipline more than you demand it.

- Trust differences in style.

- Don't sweat the small stuff.

- Trust your child's developmental process.

Daily Life: The Ground Level

With the big picture and the principles as the backdrop, let's look at how Mindful Discipline is practiced in daily life as we try to create harmony in our homes while supporting self-discipline. Our general approach to minimizing behavioral issues involves prevention through connection, meeting misbehavior by meeting the need, and allowing for messiness and mis-takes.

Prevention Through Connection

When all is going well, our parenting work is to be proactive. We call this principle "prevention through connection." By connecting with our children often, being proactive in reading their needs, and taking responsibility for meeting those needs (especially in the early years), we can drastically decrease acting out and "misbehavior." Our commitment and follow-through can make life easier for everyone. In some situations, "misbehavior" can be significantly reduced simply by the parent's proactively providing nourishment before the child instinctively moves to get attention.

So we make sure that our children are fed and get the sleep they need. We make sure they are filled up with relational nourishment—that they feel seen and respected, and know that they are an important part of the team. We also support their emerging desire for autonomy and their drive to become more competent in the ways of the world. We set boundaries that draw out their developing capacities to cooperate and navigate relationships in a healthy way. And equally as important, we help our children practice allowing their vulnerable feelings to flow, which helps them become resilient in the face of adversity. When we say no to the third cookie and they cry, we hold them lovingly, knowing that tears and experiences of futility are a key part of resilience and emotional intelligence.

Meeting Misbehavior by Meeting the Need

No matter how attuned and proactive we are about meeting our kid's needs, there will be many dissonant moments every day. It is not possible—nor is it desirable—for our children to go along with everything we say. You want your son to have his own desires, interests, and aspirations. His impulse to stand up for himself, even—or especially—when he's standing up to you, is a sign of health and indicates he is protecting his own process of individuation. Given these truths, how can we most effectively deal with his "misbehavior"? Underlying all acts of misbehavior are needs, so we must meet misbehavior by meeting the need. When we meet our children's needs, their nervous systems are emptied of the tension driving them toward gratification.

Sometimes when your son acts out, he needs to be loved unconditionally and have the goodness in him reflected and seen. Sometimes when your daughter misbehaves, she needs a subtle look that communicates your displeasure, and then she needs space to right her wrong without additional pressure. We may need to set up structures to help our children remember the bedtime routine rather than assuming they are trying to purposely aggravate us. Sometimes your five-year-old needs a firm limit—to be shown in no uncertain terms that she is not the one who gets to decide whether she can watch another movie at eight o'clock at night. These interactions each have a different flavor, but in each case the child's need is understood and met.

A child's needs are often not the same as his wants, so we have to use our mindful discernment to the best of our ability. But when you meet misbehavior by meeting the need, the behavior shifts and both you and your child are gratified—not in a shallow "I am happy to be sucking on another lollipop" way, but in ways that are deeply nourishing and that support the development of your child's confidence and her sense of being an important part of the team. The various ways that meeting her needs during acts of misbehavior can manifest in real life will be detailed in the second part of this book.

Allowing for Messiness and Mis-takes

Finally, we invariably land at times in the realm of messiness and mistakes (or mis-takes, as we call them in the context of parenting): it just comes with the territory. Even as we offer you these ideals to aim for and a variety of mindfulness awareness practices (MAPs) to help you keep your cool, please don't think for a minute that we think mis-takes are bad or wrong. We really value mis-takes and messiness. We think they play a crucial role in our children's growth and our own process of maturation. We feel that it is much better to allow some healthy flow of emotion rather than chronically suppressing feelings like frustration, anger, hurt, and disappointment in an attempt to be perfect. It is true that as parents we need to be attentive and work at becoming more and more emotionally intelligent. We don't want to overwhelm our children with too much uncontrolled emotion, or make them feel like they are primarily responsible for our feelings. But we can guarantee you that in the process of living an authentic life, mis-takes will be made. And we can equally guarantee you that this is not a problem.

Sometimes children get exactly what they need when we get pushed over our edge and raise our voices at them. These "mis-takes" have invaluable lessons contained within them, for ourselves as well as our children. Children learn that there are limits to a parent's patience, that we can only take so much abuse. This is important to learn before going out into the world where people will be less forgiving.

Also important in these messy encounters is the lesson that relational storms can be weathered, and that ruptures always culminate in repairs and in greater intimacy after we fall apart and reconnect in our humanness. Your daughter will also discover that mommy is still learning how to be self-disciplined, and this will free her from too much self-judgment and harshness when she herself becomes caught in an emotional storm. Your authentic struggle will allow your daughter to be more authentic as well, and learn how to work with her emotions in intelligent ways rather than merely suppressing them. Passion and fire go hand in hand, so we need to learn how to consciously work with them if we are to thrive.

Now that we've outlined the general Mindful Discipline approach when it comes to preventing and dealing with misbehavior, let's turn to how awareness of our own state of consciousness can help us more successfully navigate moments in which discipline is required.

States of Consciousness

When it comes to matters of discipline, the most important skill is mindful awareness—specifically to become aware of your own state of consciousness. *State of consciousness* is a term describing the patterns of energy and information running through your body in any given moment. For example, relaxing on your back deck with a cup of tea after the children have gone off to school, listening to only the sounds of birds singing, you may be experiencing a very peaceful state: body and mind are calm, attention is relaxed and open, and you are enjoying things as they come. Or, in another moment, after the principal calls and asks you to attend a meeting after school about your daughter, you may find yourself in a more agitated state: heart racing, attention narrowed to trying to guess at what happened, body tense and moving around erratically, and thinking slightly disorganized.

In the Mindful Discipline approach, we describe three general states of consciousness: reactive, responsive, and intuitive. These states represent varying degrees to which your nervous system is integrated and reflects how well your prefrontal cortex is functioning. This in turn influences the degree of emotional intelligence and resilience you are capable of in the moment. The *reactive* state is the least integrated brain state and displays the largest impairment of PFC functioning; it is characterized by less self-regulation, less impulse control, less attunement and empathy, and less self-insight and access to intuition. The highest state of PFC functioning and overall brain integration is found in the *intuitive* state. The *responsive* state is an intermediate state between the states of reactivity and intuition, and is probably the state you experience in normal moments when you are not highly stressed. Let's look at each state a little more carefully.

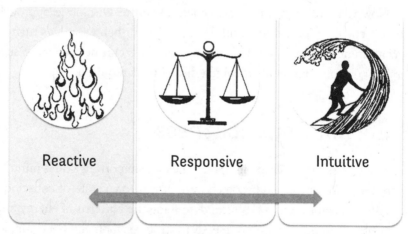

3 States of Consciousness

Figure 4: Three States of Consciousness

Reactive State

In a *reactive* state, you may find yourself tense, frustrated, or angry. This is the state when the fire alarms are going off in your emotional brain. In the reactive state, we lose our cool and act in ways that are hurtful to other people. This is where we make "mis-takes" and act out of step with how we want to parent our children. Some people react with anger and hostility in the face of stress and discomfort, some shut down and withdraw from the situation, and some become overly anxious and accommodate their children's wishes to unhealthy extremes.

These reactive strategies are hardwired into our nervous systems and are completely normal and natural. However, states of reactivity are the most dangerous to our relationships and to the prospects of living life in accord with our values. Learning to recognize that you are in a reactive state can help you immensely in becoming the parent you want to be.

Responsive State

The *responsive* state reflects higher levels of brain integration, PFC functioning, and the nine capacities it supports compared with the reactive state (see appendix A for more details). When you are in a responsive state of consciousness, you are aware of the many moving parts in any given situation and are able to flexibly respond in a way that is healthy and just. If your toddler is upset and crying because you won't let her stay at the park, you feel the discomfort of her crying in your body and your reactive urge to make it stop. But you are also aware of her right to be treated respectfully, so you control your impulse to growl, "Keep crying and I will give you something to cry about!" You are also aware of her need for a nap, and are able to start finding a respectful way to move her toward her *need* rather than giving in to her *want* to stay at the park. When in the responsive mode, you parent with skill and confidence.

Intuitive State

In some moments, we may find ourselves lucky enough to be in an *intuitive* state of consciousness. In the intuitive state, life is inherently pleasurable and full of flow. We are in touch with the preciousness of this moment and how blessed we truly are. We see our children for what they are: little beings on their own path—unique, authentic, and heading toward some unknown future to fulfill their purpose on this earth. As Khalil Gibran wrote, "Your children are not your children. They are the sons and daughters of Life's longing for itself" (1923, 17). In some moments, the beauty of this truth cracks us wide open.

In the intuitive mode, we roll with the punches easefully. We take up struggles as a dance—blending with our little sparring partner effortlessly, and fluidly finding our way to solutions without even trying. From this state, mindfulness and discipline are our very nature. The more moments we are able to live in this state, the more our families will benefit and the more fulfilling our lives will become. Because we are human, and because reactivity and responsiveness are normal, universal states of consciousness, our intuitive moments of insight and flow will arise and pass away. But having these moments—as well as remembering them with gratitude, and trusting that they'll come again—nourishes us and our children through our less sublime experiences.

Working with Your States

The reason that knowing our state of consciousness is important in any given moment is because it will guide, in general, what the most helpful course of action will be. Here are our general recommendations about parenting from each of the three states.

When you are in an *intuitive* state, trust your instincts and your intuitions. When you are graced with this state of consciousness, you will be seeing situations with great clarity and perspective. Let yourself be effortlessly guided by the natural intelligence of your heart—as Jack Kornfield calls it, the "heart that knows what is just, loving, and beautiful" (2002). And *enjoy* the pleasure and flow of this beautiful state while it lasts.

Really soak it in and let the experience sink into every cell of your body and nourish you.

When you are in a *responsive* state, continue to listen to your gut instincts and intuitions, but also use mental reflection to help evaluate what is working and what is not. There will be times when you'll go with your gut and be spot-on. And there will be other times when your instincts are off and do not hit the mark. No problem. Just reflect, re-evaluate, and try again to meet the needs of your child and the needs of the situation.

When you are in a *reactive* state, there are two likely outcomes. The first, and most ideal situation, is that you recognize that you are in a "red alert" state and simply step away from your child. You may have to say something like "We will talk about this later" or "Daddy needs a little space" before you walk away. If your partner is around, this is a good time to ask them to take over so you can recompose yourself by going for a little walk, sitting in meditation, or doing some vigorous exercise to get the frustration from locking up in your body. If no one is there to help you, try to get a little space from your child—as long as he or she is in a safe place—by walking outside, locking yourself in the bathroom, or going downstairs "to change the laundry." Once you get some space, we recommend trying one of our mindfulness awareness practices. These practices can greatly reduce your chances of "going over the edge" and doing something you might regret.

Frustration and tension are very common experiences for parents. These are usually caused by a combination of some instinctual energy arising in the body and then meeting a cap of suppression. When your child wakes you up from the dead of sleep by yelling in your face, there will likely be a burst of fear or anger that rushes through your nervous system. As you realize it is only your child doing what three-year-olds do, you suppress the impulse to yell at him or push the threat away. These natural acts of suppression can lead to a lot of bottled up frustration in the body and mind. The following mindfulness awareness practice is one safe way to help let off some steam. The next time you recognize that you are on the cusp of reactivity, duck into a bedroom or bathroom when you are able to take a mini-moment, and try this practice.

Mindfulness Awareness Practice 5:

Heat Up the Tension

On an inhale, clench your fists, face, and whole body really tightly, fully activating all your muscles and holding the tension for a full three seconds. On the exhale, make an "Aaaaahhhhh" sound in the back of your throat, letting all the tension drain out of your body down into the earth and out into the room, letting all your muscles fully relax. Inhale again and tense up all your muscles, heating up the frustration and anger as hot as you can get it for a full three seconds. And then release completely with the exhale, imagining that you are dissolving outward in all directions. At the end of the exhale, enjoy the momentary peace and spaciousness of the moment. Do this for a total of three breaths, and then rejoin your family.

This practice will not solve whatever difficulty you are facing, but it will shift you toward a responsive state of consciousness and precipitate more emotionally intelligent responses from you. You will temporarily feel a little more space and gain some perspective on the very real challenge you face. Heating up the tension can be of benefit to both you and your children.

The other possible outcome of being in the reactive state is to find yourself in that oh-so-fun swampland of messiness and mis-takes. On one hand, let's do what we can to keep it from happening too often. On the other hand, it will happen—that's life.

The best we can do when our reactivity leads us into messiness and mis-takes is try to turn manure into fertilizer for growth. As we discussed earlier, experiences of messiness and mis-takes are actually an essential part of healthy parenting; through them we prepare our children for a world in which they and other people are messy and make mis-takes and hurt others, and it's not the end of the world.

Part of recovering from our reactive behavior, reconnecting with our children, and growing together is self-compassion. It becomes really important to be able to forgive ourselves in these situations rather than continuing to judge ourselves too harshly. Guilt and shame are natural emotional reactions that indicate something has gone awry, but they are most helpful when we use them as an alert system and then let go of them. Parenting is incredibly hard. Not only are we pushed beyond our limit almost every day, but we love our children so much that it is really painful to hurt or scare them in any way. Compassion and forgiveness are invaluable responses in these heartbreaking moments. After we have lifted ourselves out of guilt and shame, we are then in a position to reconnect with our child, make amends, and become even closer in our mutual "brokenness." Once the intimacy and trust are restored, we can set some new intentions to make things go more smoothly the next time.

Being aware of our states of consciousness—whatever they happen to be—is essential to our being able to navigate our reactive states, support our responsive states, and enjoy our intuitive states. The following mindfulness awareness practice helps us build that awareness.

Mindfulness Awareness Practice 6:
Know Your State

At least three times a day—but as often as you can remember to do it—sense your current state of consciousness. Ask yourself, "Am I in a reactive state, a responsive state, or an intuitive state?"

Sense your body. How tense is it? How uncomfortable is it? Are you feeling frustrated, angry, withdrawn, or anxious? These are all clues that you may be on the cusp of, or entering into, a state of reactivity.

Check out your attention and your goals. Are you watching your child's every move like a hawk, waiting for them to do "just one more thing!"? Are you feeling really tuned out, fuzzy, or withdrawn, not wanting to be with your child at all? Are you hypervigilant and falsely effusive, trying to make sure everything goes perfect and that everyone is happy? These may be indications that you are in some degree of reactivity. If you are, it may be a good time to "heat up the tension" or to otherwise take a moment away from your child to calm and support yourself.

The value of knowing your state of consciousness is that it allows you to work with the truth of where you are in a wise and intentional way. Throughout the rest of this book we will be offering you various practices to help shift your state of consciousness where appropriate. But the first step is recognition, so begin making it a habit to know your state of consciousness.

Intimate, direct contact with our body is the key to this awareness. We know our states of consciousness primarily through sensing ourselves in the present moment. Furthermore, it is only through contact with *our own bodies* that we can experience and know the states and needs of *our children*. Neuroscientific research supports the idea that empathy arises from information coming in through our senses and affecting the currents running through our brain, nervous system, and body, after which we sense our children's states through our own bodily experience (Siegel 2007). Being attuned to our bodily experience—which reflects our unconscious knowledge of our children's states as well as our own—can allow us to *consciously* consider what a child is likely feeling: "She seems really anxious. I wonder if it is about the tournament." Putting your attention on your own body and then sensing your child with your whole being can greatly increase your ability to know her from the inside out. As your ability to sense your own body increases, you become more attuned and more empathic, and your actions arise more organically and intuitively from your naturally wise and loving heart. This practice of bodily awareness and attunement will help you put the parenting books away and trust yourself and your own inner wisdom more and more each day.

The body scan meditation, described in the mindfulness awareness practice that follows, is a time-tested practice for building bodily awareness. The technique requires focusing your awareness slowly, deliberately, and systematically on the body, from toe to head, applying moment-by-moment awareness to whatever your experience of each body part is, including awareness of sensations, emotions, and associated thoughts about the body if they arise. We recommend trying this practice as you are lying in bed at night, using this time to come back into direct contact with yourself and increase your capacity for feeling awareness.

Mindfulness Awareness Practice 7:
Body Scan

The body scan meditation is usually practiced lying down on your back (a position referred to as "rest pose" or "corpse pose" in yoga traditions), with your legs extended, feet hip-width apart, and arms by your sides with palms facing up. This is an open and receptive posture. Ideally the environment will be a warm, safe, and quiet location that will provide minimal distractions.

Begin by forming a clear intention for this practice: "May I learn to listen to my body with greater care" or "May this practice help me be more present as a parent." Once you have an intention, silently repeat it to yourself, and then let it go, focusing your awareness on the breath. Feel the breath move in and out of the body, riding the waves of your own breathing from moment to moment, and noticing how you don't have to think about breathing; you can simply feel it.

When you are in touch with the flow of the breath in the body, direct your attention to the toes of your left foot. Pay close attention to any sensations (or lack of sensation) in this area of your body. Don't worry if you get distracted or have a hard time feeling anything at all in your toes; as soon as you notice your mind wandering, gently return focus to your toes, noticing without judgment whatever your experience of that area of your body may be.

Next, shift your attention to the rest of the left foot, including the sensations of pressure in the heel touching the surface you are resting on. When you are ready move to the left ankle. And, in this way, move slowly and systematically through every region of your body. The order of the scan can be as follows: the toes of the left foot...bottom of the left foot and heel...upper foot...ankle...lower leg...knee...thigh...hip; the toes of the right foot...bottom of the right foot and heel...upper foot... ankle...lower leg...knee...thigh...hip; the whole pelvis...lower back... abdomen; the upper back...rib cage...chest; the shoulder blades and the shoulders; the left fingers...hand...arm; the right fingers...hand...arm; the neck...throat...head...face.

For each area, check in to see what sensations are available to your awareness and dwell with those sensations, also noticing any other experience as you pay attention to different body parts, such as the holding of tension, or emotions and associations that may arise. Notice any tendencies to rush ahead or dwell longer on certain areas. When moving from each area, imagine with an out-breath releasing your focus and allowing that area to dissolve from awareness as you move on to the next.

Finally, dwell for some time at the very top of your head. Imagine you have a blowhole there like a whale or a dolphin, where you can draw air in and out. See if you can draw the air in through the blowhole and feel it travel through your entire body to the very bottoms of your feet, then back in through the feet and out through the top of your head as you exhale. Perhaps feel a warmth flow through your body as your entire body breathes as a whole system, feeling complete and content. Feel a sense of the breath flowing in and out, the whole body held in your kind awareness.

When it is time to end the body scan, notice the effects of the practice on your mind and body. Notice if you feel different than you did when you began. It is helpful to again reflect on your intention for this practice; for example, "to be a more mindful parent" or "to take care of myself." Finally, thank yourself for taking this time and giving yourself this gift of awareness.

The body scan practice is valuable both because it is soothing to have mindful contact with the direct experience of ourselves, and because it is through the body that we come to know our own emotional states and the states and needs of our children.

Summary

The Mindful Discipline approach is to decrease acting-out behaviors by prevention through connection, meeting misbehavior by meeting the need, and allowing room for messiness and mis-takes. Central to each of these outward approaches to discipline is the inner practice of knowing our own state of consciousness and responding accordingly. Embodying self-discipline not only teaches our children the most about respect and responsibility, it is also our own practice and path to becoming a more authentic and loving human being.

> The greatest gift you can give someone is to get yourself together.
>
> —Wendy Palmer, *The Intuitive Body*

5.

RELATIONSHIP

The Source of Nourishment

Parenthood is above all a relationship, not a skill to be acquired. Attachment is not a behavior to be learned, but a connection to be sought.

—Gordon Neufeld and Gabor Maté, *Hold on to Your Kids*

Nature, in its infinite wisdom, has arranged for young social mammals to be born into the loving care of mature adults. Every social mammal has hardwired circuits within her brain that mediate this relationship. Psychologists and neuroscientists call this relationship "attachment." It is not something we need to learn to do; this relationship is instinctual and intuitive (see appendix B for more details).

Instinctively, our young look to us for protection, care, and guidance, which we as parents are naturally moved to provide. The purpose of this mutual attachment is to meet the needs of our children robustly enough that they both survive *and* thrive. When we meet our children's needs on a regular basis, their survival drive can rest and their energy can be redirected into learning and growing—thriving. The safe and loving environment we create enables children to function better, to experience more joy and fulfillment, and to grow most easefully into self-actualized individuals. Our job is not to figure out which neurons need to be connected up to create emotional intelligence, self-discipline, and resilience, but to create the environment that supports the developmental plan of nature.

When you center and trust yourself, you will listen more deeply to your intuition and become more attuned to your child's needs. Your relationship with yourself directly impacts how you relate to your child. Right relationship is the key to caring for children, guiding them toward self-discipline, and creating harmony in our home. As Gordon Neufeld says, "It's not what we do, but *who we are* to our children that matters most" (personal communication, 2012).

How Relationships Affect Children

In preceding chapters, we have referred several times to the three main parenting styles—authoritarian, permissive, and authoritative. There is a significant body of research on these styles and their effects on children, starting with the work of Diana Baumrind (discussed in Grolnick 2009).

In her research, Baumrind identified two primary dimensions that were predictive of the child's well-being and his capacity for emotionally intelligent self-discipline: the responsiveness and demandingness of the parents. *Responsiveness* means the parent is able to recognize the child as his own person and to respond in a way that reflects understanding of the child's desires, feelings, and beliefs, and communicates to the child, "I see you, hear you, and feel you, and will do my best to meet your needs." *Demandingness* involves asking the child to contribute to the harmony of the family and to her self-care to the degree that she is developmentally capable. It is a term that feels abrasive, but actually means asking your children to try and do their best to be respectful and responsible.

The three parenting styles can be understood in terms of these dimensions. Authoritarian parenting is low in responsiveness and high in demandingness. In Baumrind's longitudinal research, these children in preschool were moody, unhappy, and more aimless, and did not get along well with other children. By age eight and nine, they were lower in achievement motivation and social assertiveness. In the teen years, they continued to be low in achievement motivation and high in seeking adult approval, and they lacked individuation and autonomy. They were also found to have higher rates of drug use than children in the authoritative parenting group.

Permissive parenting is high in responsiveness and low in demand-ingness. The preschool children in this group lacked impulse control, were more self-centered, and were low in achievement motivation as well. By ages eight and nine, they scored lower in both cognitive and social competencies. And in adolescence, these teens continued to be low in achievement motivation and competence, exhibited lower degrees of self-regulation, and had higher rates of drug use than children in both the authoritarian and authoritative groups.

Authoritative parenting is high in both responsiveness and demand-ingness. The preschoolers of this group were energetic, socially outgoing, and independent. The eight- and nine-year-olds were high in achieve-ment motivation, and friendly and socially responsive. The teens of this group were highly individuated, mature, and strong in self-regulation, and they remained highly motivated toward achievement.

The take-away from this research is that recognizing your child as her own person with her own desires, feelings, and beliefs—and com-municating to her this attunement—is essential for mental health and mature development. Equally as important is to set clear boundaries and expectations: to lovingly but firmly set our expectations of respectful and responsible behaviors at age-appropriate levels. The combination of attunement and expectation helps our children become more emotion-ally and socially intelligent. And most importantly, we communicate to them that the relationship is solid *no matter what*: We say, in effect, "There is no misbehavior or misstep that will ever separate us. Don't you worry. I will always be here for you and help you find your way." This is what helps our children bloom into their best and brightest selves.

Loving Hierarchy: The Ideal Relationship for Children

What this research suggests is that children benefit most from an author-itative relationship that is hierarchical. We refer to this relationship as a *loving hierarchy* to emphasize the asymmetry *and* the heart contained within nature's plan. You as the parent are responsible for protecting, caring for, and guiding your child; not the other way around. The parent-child relationship is *not* primarily a democracy, and children are definitely not meant to be in charge. If you flatten or invert this natural developmental plan—making the child an equal in decision making or, worse, putting them in charge—you will create trouble, both for your home life and for your child's development (Neufeld and Maté 2004).

Discussions of hierarchy and power differentials can make some of us uncomfortable. But the abuse of our power and the loving exercise of it are not the same thing at all. When we confidently take up our role as parents to protect and to care for our children above all else, then they relax into their dependent mode, look to us for guidance, and want to be good for us. This is not the display of dominating power over our children, but rather an embodiment of authority that gives us the inherent and appropriate power to simultaneously nourish our children and create harmony in our homes. If you want your children to

Retain a soft heart that is the source of emotional intelligence

Become resilient in the face of adversity

Benefit from your experience and loving guidance

Develop beyond self-centeredness into the truth of interdependence

Remain sweet, endearing, and a joy to be around, and

Grow into their full potential

then a loving hierarchical relationship is necessary.

The first and most important distinction in our discussion of hierarchy in relationship is that there are *natural hierarchies* and there are *dominance hierarchies* (Wilber 2000). Let's start with natural hierarchies. Everywhere you look in the social-mammalian world you will see cubs, pups, and children arranged in a hierarchical relationship with their mother. The momma bear is in the *alpha* position, which means that she is responsible for protecting, caring for, and guiding her cubs into maturity. The cubs are attached in the *dependent* mode: they accept the protection, care, and guidance of their mother until they reach maturity. This is the natural and intelligent order of things—the mature caring for the immature—and it does not work well if reversed.

Human children have the same attachment brain—located in the limbic system—as all other social mammals. The attachment brain has two modes in it: the alpha mode and the dependent mode (Neufeld and Maté 2004). This part of our brain always wants to know, "Which position am I in with this person?" Remember William Golding's *Lord of the Flies*? The story of that novel illustrates how, if you remove the adults, children will instinctively move into hierarchical relationships: that is how the attachment brain works.

Often, parents hear the word "alpha" and stop listening. We have all witnessed such atrocious abuses at the hands of an alpha that we want nothing to do with hierarchy. But abuse is indicative of a *dominance hierarchy* and represents a distortion of the natural alpha instinct. Instead of protecting, caring for, and guiding the dependent member, a person in the alpha position who has become hardened—or remains selfish and immature, or is perhaps both—will use and abuse the dependent member for her own purposes. This distortion is what we all fear and is the reason some of us believe that hierarchy should have no place in our home.

And yet, if you watch any mother bear in the wild, you will see the embodiment of a loving hierarchy. One day while watching a nature show, I (Chris) saw this play out very clearly. A momma bear was letting her cubs roam around, frolic, and play, and was quietly keeping a watchful eye on them. At one point, they began to encroach on a large male's fishing spot in the river. She called out a couple of warnings to them to back off, but the cubs continued to play, ignoring her gentle requests. Finally she ran over to them and gave them an earful— "Rrrrooooooooaaarrrr!" The cubs scrambled up the bank—tails between their legs—and back to the safety of the field above the river. The mother lumbered over to them, completely relaxed, having said her piece. The cubs sidled over to her with kisses, she rolled over, and they climbed on top and cuddled up.

The roar was a loving demand for *their* sake. The purpose was not to control, to hurt, or to manipulate the cubs because of some old trauma from the momma bear's childhood. It was loud and clear, but clean. The whole incident was over in seconds and the reunion was easeful. You just don't see young animals in the wild expressing postures of, "You can't tell me what to do. You're not the boss of me!" (except when the young males are finding their alpha voice and are about to head out on their own). Their parents act in ways that keep the brains of their young registering the natural order of things: a loving hierarchy is what nature needs to do its work. In the womb of right relationship, nature will ripen our children in due time.

Human children mature optimally in the same way. We have an especially long period of dependency—especially in this day and age, because of our increasingly complex culture—and need to be held in a loving hierarchy long enough to develop and become proficient in navigating our lives on our own. So take the lead for meeting your child's needs. Instead of pushing her to become independent, invite her to depend on you. The maturational drive for autonomy kicks in only after the physical and relational needs have been satiated. You are responsible first and foremost for bringing her nervous system to a state of rest. We don't dangle the carrot out on a stick and make a child chase us around the yard for her dinner. We instinctively know this will keep her instincts revved up in a constant state of pursuit and make her insecure. The same is true for relational nourishment. Aim to take the lead and, as Gordon Neufeld puts it, "provide more than is being pursued" (2010, 41). Help your child relax, knowing that you are in the lead and will take care of meeting her needs. Then, and only then, will her natural drive for autonomy kick into gear in a healthy way.

Democracy is a later developmental capacity of the brain, and only emerges properly after a child's dependency needs are met. The capacity to be democratic in our thinking and interactions is one of the hallmarks of maturity and requires that our prefrontal cortex develop over many years to support these capacities. But the prefrontal cortex does not develop optimally unless the child can safely attach in the dependent mode with a loving caregiver. The roots of a natural hierarchy must be cultivated first before the fruits of democratic thinking will emerge.

Hierarchy, Emotional Intelligence, and Resilience

So, as Baumrind's research shows us, hierarchy is important, but there must be responsiveness and love inherent in the guidance (Grolnick 2009). Why is this true? How does it work? First and foremost, children need to feel that all of their desires, emotions, and perspectives are welcome. We need the full range of instinctual impulses and emotions to be preserved if we are to later develop the capacity to recognize and regulate them. The capacities of recognition and regulation take years to develop in a person, but the first, necessary step is allowing *emotional flow*.

Emotional flow entails allowing the natural shifts within us to unfold, and to inform and ready us for a course of action. Emotion can be understood as "e"nergy translated into "motion." When your child gets excited about eating some of the cake she just spotted on top of the fridge, that is emotion in flow. You can see the excitement and desire on her face and in her body movements, and hear it in her voice. Allowing desire to flow is important for preserving passion and vitality in her life.

If our children get the message that we don't like their excitement, frustration, or anger, they will be moved to repress these emotions in order to preserve their connection with us. This hampers the development of emotional intelligence and resilience over time, and is a reason that authoritarian relationships tend to not support healthy self-discipline. Authoritarian parenting leads to unhealthy suppression of instinct and emotion.

But allowing emotional flow does not mean our children can do whatever they want. It is important for children to begin to see the difference between what we feel inside—how we are moved by our emotion—and what *is* and what *is not* an appropriate expression of our impulses in different environments. This of course takes years to develop (anyone still eating cake before dinner?), but it starts with us allowing our children's emotions to be expressed and reflecting to them that we understand where they are coming from.

In the early years it is mostly *our* responsibility to help our children become regulated and guide them toward appropriate expressions. For example, if your three-year-old is feeling very powerful and energetic, bouncing off the walls and getting dangerously close to breaking some of your valuables, it becomes your responsibility to work with the situation in a way that preserves the flow of his wildness, while protecting your valuables and the other people in the house. In this situation, you might move the breakables to a safe place or say, "I see you are really excited right now. Let's go outside where you can be as wild as you want without breaking anything." An intuitive response like this preserves the connection and emotional flow, and protects Grandma's china from being shattered.

As our children get older, we can increasingly explain to them (and hopefully model) our behavioral expectations. When children begin to understand the structures and guidelines for healthy living, they can then begin to practice self-regulation and feel some degree of self-efficacy in various environments. This is one aspect of healthy self-esteem that does not require our constant praise, but becomes self-generating. Confidence arises naturally from competence, and without some guidance regarding cultural norms and expectations, children are left handicapped in this respect. When a child is allowed to continue with an "anything goes" attitude for too long, she begins to suffer the natural consequences of being impulsive and self-centered. These children are often not invited to the birthday parties and sleepovers, and tend to become more isolated over time from the community. This is naturally upsetting to a child who, through no fault of his own, has not been guided into his own capacities for self-regulation.

In addition to allowing and reflecting emotional flow, as well as guidance toward appropriate expression, there is a third gift we need to give our children: support for autonomy and competence. As we will discuss more fully in chapter seven, children need room to practice life skills on their own or with just enough support so they still feel like they are at the steering wheel. An image that perfectly captures this aspect of autonomy support is the new phenomenon of the balance bike.

For those of you not familiar with the balance bike, it is a small bike that has no pedals or training wheels, but sits close enough to the ground that young children can use their feet for both locomotion and balance. Children start riding this bike around two to three years old, and are routinely riding a pedal bike by three to four. This is much earlier than with children who use training wheels. With training wheels, the child lumbers along, rocking side to side, and the training wheels catch them and keep them balanced. This "puts them to sleep," in the sense that they don't have to pay too much attention to keeping themselves upright, and actually don't get much practice in doing so. With the balance bike, the implicit message is clear: "you are responsible for your balance." Because of this, children on a balance bike pay attention and balance themselves. The child gets practice with steering her own ship.

In this way, it becomes important for us to find ways to allow our children to practice steering and finding solutions to their own problems wherever safe and possible. As parents, we are still in charge, but we stay out of the way while they practice. The momma bear lets the children frolic, getting into a little trouble here and there while developing their skills, but steps in when things are getting too dangerous. One of today's parenting phenomena that's unhealthy for children is what's often referred to as "helicopter parenting." This is where the parents take too much autonomy from their kids, protecting them at every turn so that the child never has to experience the "fall." Protecting our children from failure leaves them unequipped to deal with life on their own. These children often feel fragile and relatively incapable. This is partly from a lack of real world experience and partly from the implicit messages they have received from their parents: "You can't handle it on your own. I will do it for you." The loving hierarchy offers balance, giving space to our children to experience all of life—the successes and the failures—while always making sure as best we can that our children are safe and pro-tected from serious harm.

Over time, a child who grows up with responsiveness, boundaries, and autonomy support will begin to develop emotional intelligence. He will become capable of having mixed perspectives and feelings by around the age of five to seven years (Neufeld and Maté 2004). This development of the child's "on the other hand" feelings will eventually allow him to authentically choose the most appropriate response more effectively than would a rigid set of rules mechanically applied to all situations. Impulse control and response flexibility begin to arise from the discordant feelings within his own wise and loving heart: "I want to hit my sister, but I also love her and don't want to hurt her"; "I am afraid of failing, but I really want to play ball with the big boys." Ultimately, you want your child to responsibly self-regulate by listening to his own internal compass, rather than doing it because it was a rule written on the whiteboard.

Facets of Healthy Relationship

Within the larger context of a loving hierarchy, there are four additional facets of our relationship with our children. These configurations span the range of interactions we'll have with our children, from undivided attention to support for their autonomy and competence to a firm exercise of our parental authority. They are 1) special time, 2) child-led time, 3) democratic decision making, and 4) benevolent dictatorship.

Special Time

Special time is a period of time set aside during the day when we drop everything and give our child our 100 percent, undivided attention. Here the intention is to saturate and satiate them: to bring them to a state of utter fulfillment (Wipfler 2006). Special time is incredibly nourishing for children and the relationship as a whole. My (Chris's) son Kai and I like to go on "big-boy" hikes and then stop at our favorite burger joint for fries and a milkshake. I put the phone away. If we listen to music it is something we both like and enjoy together. Our one-on-one time together has become especially important since the arrival of his little brother.

It's not the amount of time we spend together, but the quality. Even ten or fifteen minutes per day can fill our children up with relational nourishment. Give more if you are able, but even this small effort to set aside this intentional one-on-one time for sweetness, laughter, and intimacy will go a long way to promoting a better mood as well as more teamwork and cooperation in the home.

Child-Led Time

It is also important to sometimes let your child orchestrate the play while you follow *his* lead. This gives him some practice in the alpha position, which is an important life skill to develop. When we allow children periods of time to "be the boss," they begin to learn how to be a kind and loving boss: they learn that respect and responsibility are a part of leadership.

On our hikes, I let Kai lead us. He is responsible for deciding when to walk, when to rest, and when to stop and eat our snacks. I occasionally give him some emotional feedback, like "I am a little worried about going off trail. What if we get lost?" I stay clearly in the dependent position and wait for him to reassure me—"It's all right daddy"—or tell me how he plans on making sure we don't get lost. He loves being in the lead as his natural disposition is a little more on the alpha side (just like his daddy).

It has been really good for our relationship and I experience less push-back from him when I regularly allow him periods of leading. When we go a few days without giving him these periods of leading, we all pay the price with his pushback and obstinance. Again, we suggest at least ten or fifteen minutes per day of child-led time. More time will likely benefit children who have a strong alpha personality, but this will have to be balanced with firm boundaries at other appropriate times in the day.

Democratic Decision Making

Increasingly, as children get older, they also need more experience with democratic decision making. The Collins English Dictionary defines *democracy* as "the practice or spirit of social equality" (11th ed., s.v. "democracy"). In parenting, these interactions are where we work to find a "win-win," take turns, or take a vote and the majority decision holds. When riding in the car, my (Chris's) son Kai will often want to hear a good song over and over again. Sometimes I play it for him again because it makes him so happy, but after the third round of "Wake Up" by Arcade Fire, I am ready to move on. I say, "Okay, we are going to take turns now. I get to pick the next song, then Bodhi"—my other son—"and then it's your turn again." There are many simple ways like this to practice democracy. Being at the top of the hierarchy does not mean that we get to choose the song every time. However, letting our child choose every time is also not very reflective of how relationships actually work. Teaching our children to compromise, to recognize that we all have different needs and desires and can dance our way to win-win solutions, is an essential part of parenting. Observe your interactions with your children and you will see how you do this instinctively.

These democratic-style interactions communicate the following: "In certain ways, you and I are on equal footing. We are both human beings with needs who deserve to be respected and considered. I will do my best to take turns and negotiate when possible." Cooperation and collaboration help our children develop empathy and problem-solving skills, and allow them to practice in the give-and-take of daily life.

Benevolent Dictatorship

The fourth facet in a loving hierarchy relationship is the benevolent dictatorship. This aspect is called forth when we need to draw a firm boundary and clearly state what will happen despite our child's strongest objections. There are times when we are clear that something is not in our child's best interest and we must simply hold the line, firmly and lovingly. When your twelve-year-old asks you to go to an unsupervised party, it is not unkind for the answer to be "No." When your child wants a fourth cookie before bed, it does not damage the relationship to unilaterally decide against it. In fact, as you will see in chapter nine, it actually deepens and strengthens the relationship. You are the momma bear; trust your naturally wise and loving heart and claim your loving authority, and your child will trust you.

The Yin and Yang of Mindful Discipline

What this all boils down to is that children need both yin and yang elements of relational nourishment. In the Chinese system, the yin element is open, receptive, and allowing of the flow of energy as it is. The yang element is more directional, guiding, and aimed at a particular intention. In the Mindful Discipline approach, we identify five elements, two of which are "yin" elements, and two of which are "yang" elements. The yin elements communicate, "You are perfect as you are," and the yang elements communicate, "and there is still room for improvement." It may sound paradoxical but both are true: children are perfect exactly as they are *and* they have a long way to go in terms of their development.

We refer to unconditional love (chapter six) and space (chapter seven) as the yin elements of relationship in the context of Mindful Discipline. *Unconditional love* involves putting the connection above all else and showing our child that she can never fall out of our grace. *Space* is where we give the child plenty of room to *be* and *become* fully herself. The power of receiving these yin elements is that our child's instinctual and emotional system remains open rather than repressed and distorted. Left intact to develop and unfold according to the developmental plan, instincts and emotions increasingly become recognizable to the child, allowing for greater self-regulation. Feeling your respect and your love, she retains a basic trust in life and a sense of her own inherent value as a person.

The two yang elements of parenting are mentorship (chapter eight) and healthy boundaries (chapter nine). *Mentorship* involves modeling desirable behaviors and showing our children disciplined ways of being in the world. Children learn from the people they love. Showing children how to work with frustration and anger in a constructive manner, being consistently respectful to all living beings, and displaying ways to repair our missteps both provides nourishment for their developing psyches and scaffolds their minds in the direction of emotional health.

The other yang element—setting clear, *healthy boundaries*—provides essential nourishment for her capacities of impulse control and adaptability. Part of our job as parents is to help children ride the edge of their emerging capacities, work at drawing on their resources, and grow beyond their fear into their fullness. Yes, a young sapling needs adequate protection, but it also becomes more resilient from having to stretch a little toward the sun or toward the water lying deep in the ground. The yang aspects nourish resilience through development of an emotional heartiness.

Mis-takes do not fit as easily into one category or the other, but healthy recovery from our missteps requires both elements. When a mistake occurs we must start by accepting the truth of the situation (yin) and then move in the direction of repair and reconnection (yang). In this way, our children experience an integration of both elements as we model recovery from our foibles.

It is important to be loving alphas to our children—to remember that it is our responsibility to read their needs and respond appropriately. "Feeling them from our heart" is one way to experience this; the mindfulness awareness practice that follows can help. A good time to try it would be the next time you are at the park, relaxing on the bench while your child is playing, or in a similar situation.

Mindfulness Awareness Practice 8:
Feeling From the Heart

Inhale through the nose and imagine filling your heart with warm breath. On the exhale, allow the warm breath to flow out straight from your heart, out toward your child playing over there. Then draw the breath back toward yourself, bringing with it some sense of your child's texture in this moment. Maybe you feel her contentment. Maybe her focus. Maybe she feels a little daydreamy. Whatever you feel her experiencing, breathe that in through the front of your chest, allowing it to land in your heart as a felt sense. Repeat this a few times until you begin to intimately feel your child's shape and texture.

Is she needing anything right now? Some attention and connection? Some space? Or is her state something that can nourish you instead?

Do whatever you want with the directly experiential information you get when you practice feeling your child from your heart. But it is already enough to simply breathe your child in and experience her deeply. This is a practice that can be done silently anywhere at any time, and can bring you into a more intimate communion with everyone and everything around you.

Summary

It is the relationship you have with your child that supports the natural emergence of emotional intelligence, self-discipline, and resilience. When you establish a loving hierarchy and take responsibility for meeting the needs of your child, you provide the best environment for him to grow up whole, authentic, and kind. It is not what you do, but who you are to your child—a loving alpha who dances flexibly between various relational expressions to respond to your child's present-moment needs—that matters most. The love that binds you will be your guide.

> The understanding of relationship is infinitely more important than the search for any plan of action.

—Jiddu Krishnamurti, *On Relationship*

Part 2

The Five Essential Elements of Mindful Discipline

6.

UNCONDITIONAL LOVE

Preserving Trust and Inherent Value

Love me when I least deserve it, because that is when I need it most.

—Swedish proverb

Kyle's mother asked him to please pick up the toys before dinner, and went back to cooking. Kyle is seven years old and has a habit of dumping out piles of toys in the living room and leaving them there. About ten minutes later, seeing no progress has been made on the toy cleanup, Mom felt a welling-up of irritation. She put a pause between her irritation and barking orders, and took two deep breaths. In that time, her impulse to yell changed to an instinctual desire to reconnect first: they had been distant lately. Kyle turned around and saw her standing there. Immediately he remembered the clean-up request but stood still, waiting for her to say something. Mom walked over to Kyle, kneeled down, and gave him a big hug that lasted for two deep breaths. When they released, she looked into his eyes and said, "I love you, sweetheart." "I love you too, mom," he replied. She gave a little glance at the messy room and said, "It is almost dinner time," and turned and went back to cooking. As she was stirring the sauce, she could hear the toys being put away in the living room, felt a sense of relief, and smiled.

What Is Unconditional Love?

Love is one of those concepts that is difficult to pin down to a simple definition. Part of the challenge is its subjective nature; it is something we feel inside us, and that feeling is often unique and personal. Maureen Hawkins beautifully captured how love affects us as parents when she wrote, "Before you were conceived, I wanted you. Before you were born, I loved you. Before you were here an hour, I would die for you. This is the miracle of love" (Canfield 2000, 103).

Love is partly a feeling state that affects the way energy and information course through our minds and brains. In general, people report that they feel more open and soft, especially in the front of their chest, when they feel love. We often open into an expanded sense of awareness, an increased sensitivity to the states of others, and a natural flow of kindness. The inner feelings of love seem to motivate us and increase our capacity to care for others. On the days we are "feeling the love," there is nothing we wouldn't do for our children. When the love is flowing between us, we gladly go the extra mile for them even at great cost to ourselves. Love carries us beyond our self-centered tendencies.

Now let's turn to the word "unconditional." When we offer something unconditionally, we offer it without any qualifications. When it comes to unconditional love, this means that we love our children—and more importantly, that we express our love in ways that feel loving to *them*—no matter what their behavior or level of performance is. Our children need to feel us saying, "There is no mistake, no acting out, and no failure that will stop me from loving and caring for you. I will be here for you *no matter what*." When our children feel that our love for them is unconditional, they relax into their best selves.

How Unconditional Love Nourishes

The more our child experiences an uninterrupted flow of care and connection, the less fear and anxiety she experiences, and the more she implicitly trusts that things will work out. The more she sees herself reflected in our loving eyes, the more likely she is to retain a natural sense of dignity (see figure 5). The preservation of basic trust and inherent value is among the most important gifts we can give to our children.

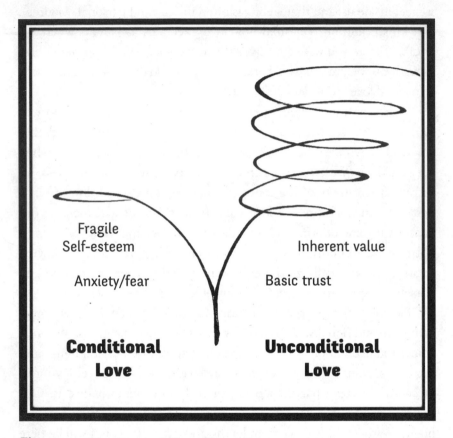

Figure 5: The Fruits of Unconditional Love

Basic Trust

When we provide our children with unconditional love, they retain a *basic trust* in reality and in themselves. Our attunement to their needs allows their natural state of relaxation to remain dominant. The fewer and less severe the disruptions and misattunements, the stronger their confidence in reality will be.

There will be times when we do not perfectly anticipate our child's needs. This is not a problem. In fact there is a level of frustration—called *optimal frustration*—that is necessary for healthy development. Every infant has instincts and capacities to signal to her caregivers when she has a need that is not being met. When we finally get the message and respond to her signals—picking her up if she wants to be held, or feeding her if she is hungry—her nervous system will again come to a state of rest and her basic trust is reaffirmed. In this way, she also comes to trust her instincts as part of the functioning of reality. This cycle—the flow of inner desire, communication of that desire, and fulfillment—is the basis for our child coming to trust herself, and in particular, trusting that her inner world of desires and emotions can guide her successfully throughout her life. Basic trust is the foundation of emotional intelligence.

If we instead communicate to our little ones, "I will only respond to you when you are sweet or nice, when you settle down, are not crying, or are not angry," then they begin to distrust themselves and their inner world of motivation and emotion. This leads to a loss of basic trust in reality and in the natural movements of their own feelings. This *conditional* love pushes the child's nervous system increasingly over to the survival side, where fear and anxiety become predominant. Repeated experiences of neglect or control lead to a more shaky sense of self, and defensive reactions begin to characterize the child's personality in place of authenticity. Inner feelings of insecurity and frustration lead to more acting-out behaviors, a poorer capacity for self-regulation, and less motivation to be respectful and responsible with her behavior.

Inherent Value

Part of developing a healthy sense of self occurs through a process psychologists call *mirroring*. We all have an innate need to be seen—and not as someone would like us to be, but rather *as we are*. Children look to our faces and our bodily responses to see "Am I welcome here? Can I be as I am? Can I feel and express what I feel?" Your child wants to know that she is understood, that her experience and her life matter to you. When our love is unconditional, the child simply retains a sense of the *inherent value* that she was born with. This is not a conscious thought like, "I am valuable," but rather an implicit sense of the goodness and rightness of her existence. Look at any four-month-old baby; do you see any trace of shame in her eyes? No, she simply shines like the gift that she is, pulling on those newfound toes of hers. Inherent value is not something that is given; it is a human birthright to be preserved.

This is decidedly not self-esteem building. The self-esteem movement, while well intended, has been misguided by the idea that self-esteem is something that you can create from the outside through positive phrases and slogans: "You are so special"; "You are so smart"; "You can do and be anything you can imagine." This pumping up of our children's self-images has led to a whole host of problems like excessive self-focus, anxiety, inflated feelings of superiority or deflated feelings of inferiority, and an inability to assume adult responsibilities (Young-Eisendrath 2008). Too much focus on self-image communicates to a child that he is a thing that you are shaping, and that that thing is valuable only when it is positive, special, or accomplished. How confusing it must be when the child sometimes feels anger and hatred, or recognizes that he is not always the best, or when he discovers that there are actually natural limits in life to who and what he can be. Accepting ourselves in our totality—the good, the bad, and the ugly—is a key ingredient to a rich and fulfilling life.

It is important to help our children know that life is a process with ups and downs and all-arounds, and that none of these assessments changes the mystery and beauty that we are. A combination of unconditional love and straight-up feedback about what works and what does not keeps our children's resilient nature and inherent sense of value intact. If we aim to preserve their sense of inherent value, we

Relax and take the ups and downs in stride

Give space to enjoy their own achievements

Provide growth-mindset feedback (see appendix D)

Emphasize our common humanity and interdependence

Allow them (and ourselves) to make mis-takes

On the other hand, if we believe we have to pump up our children's self-esteem, we are likely to

Overwork trying to make everything positive

Praise them to excess

Provide fixed-image praise (see appendix D)

Emphasize being *special*

Overprotect them

Pumping up self-esteem has the unintended effect of pushing the child's psyche over to the survival side, where he is inherently more anxious and has a fragile self-image. Thus, if you must praise, keep it to a minimum and make it specific; for example, "I like the alliteration here" as opposed to "Great essay!" Also it is more effective to focus your comments on strategy and effort rather than blanket praise (Pink 2009). Focusing on common humanity and interdependence will help your child avoid the "self-esteem trap" (Young-Eisendrath 2008). And most important, let your child mix it up with life and make mis-takes. In this way, you will help him see himself as a *process* and become a courageous, lifelong learner (see appendix D for more explanation of these concepts).

Unconditional Love in Everyday Life

There are plenty of opportunities to provide our children with a sense that they are unconditionally loved every day. Whether through your words and deeds, or simply through that look in your eyes that reflects how much you treasure them, allow your body to emanate the depths of your unconditional love for your precious little ones. These moments are incredibly nourishing for both you and your children.

I (Chris) remember one such day at the park, when my boys, Kai and Bodhi, were playing in the sand. Feeling lucky to have a minute of peace and quiet, I began to follow my breath, breathing in and out of my heart: filling it up on the inhale, and then imagining the warm breath flowing out from my chest in all directions on the exhale. As I was mindfully breathing, Bodhi's eyes caught mine and we shared a sweet moment of quiet contact. Smiling, Bodhi went back to digging and I went back to my breathing. Suddenly I began to experience a fullness to the park that was not there just seconds before. It was like the entire park was filled with a thick, warm presence. I felt my body and mind soften. Just at that moment, Kai came over to ask me something. He started his sentence, but about three or four words in he paused and looked at me. "What are you doing, daddy?" he asked with a smile. I replied, "Just looking at my sweet boy," and gently moved a stray strand of hair from his eyes. Kai looked at me for a moment, his eyes now soft and open, and sank into my lap. I pulled him up and held him against my chest just like I did when he was a baby. The fullness of the moment brought tears to my eyes as I felt the fleeting preciousness of this "now."

When They Stumble

Moments of piercing sweetness are lovely, but just as integral to demonstrating our unconditional love are moments when our children fall short, or misbehave. It's essential that we make sure our children feel our love *especially* when they seem not to have earned it. When your daughter strikes out in her baseball game, meet her eyes with the same love you would have if she got a hit. Be attuned and sensitive to how she feels about not having got a hit, but hold a place in your heart and in your way of being for the love that never fluctuates with the score.

When your son brings home bad grades, start by sitting on the couch with him in silence. Put your arm around him. Check in with him—ask how *he* feels about it. Put the love front and center so he feels you are on his side, that you believe in him. You can, and should, talk about what happened and how to do better the next semester. But he is much more likely to improve in a sustained and meaningful way with your support and encouragement, rather than threats and intimidation.

Create a Culture of Respect and Cooperation

If we treat our children kindly and respectfully, this will go a long way in eliciting respect and kindness from them. If, conversely, we are rude, rough, and disrespectful to our children, we will precipitate negative feelings in them that end up causing a vicious cycle of resentment, retaliation, and revenge. Bringing love and kindness to our interactions as often as possible will help create an upward, positive spiral in place of a downward, vicious cycle. This upward spiral promotes increasing cooperation, teamwork, and the desire to support each other toward happiness and fulfillment. So ask nicely. Say please and thank you. Be gracious and appreciative. Speak to and treat your children like you would a friend. Take care not to lose your manners around your children.

Satisfy Their Need for Connection

Hug your child first thing when she comes into the room. And make sure she is the one who lets go. To adequately relax her drive for connection, you must not merely meet her need, but you must provide more nourishment than is being pursued (Neufeld and Maté 2004). When you simply "parent on demand"—giving her attention and hugs only when she asks you for them—she remains responsible for initiating the action and for getting her needs met. But in order to be truly fulfilled—to be brought to rest from a sympathetically driven activated state of pursuit—she must be in the dependent, receptive position. This means she needs you to initiate the care and to provide "more than is being pursued."

Discernment is always important as well. In some moments having connection initiated is what is needed; at other times space will be called for. It is our job to feel what nourishment is most needed for a given child in a particular moment.

Be Authentic

Intending to unconditionally love our children is not about faking it. Our children can feel when we are being authentic and honest, and when we are manipulating our emotions and forcing a false affect. Sometimes we are simply angry, disappointed, frustrated, or hurt. That is okay; we do not need to mask it with false effusiveness. Most important is for our children to feel congruence between how we actually feel and what we are expressing. This increases their trust in us and their confidence in accurately reading the feelings of others.

So our invitation is to do what you can to make room for your emotions, but also communicate to your child that the relationship is solid. Although it is challenging to hold to both truths at the same time, you can say to your child, "I love you *and* I am angry right now. What you did was hurtful and I did not deserve to be treated that way. But we will get through this together."

Through repeated experiences of staying connected through tough times, children learn two things. First, they learn that their behavior does impact other people. It is important for your child to see that when he says, "I don't love you," it hurts. And yet, it is also important that he realizes that even though he has hurt you, you will not abandon him. When the tether of your love remains present even in—and *especially* in—emotionally turbulent times, your child will become more committed to becoming the best person he can be. And he will make the effort not for the sake of a trophy or a certificate or some conditional applause or praise, but *to maximize the flow of love* between you.

Celebrate with Them

Refrain from the desire to pump up your child's self-esteem. We have grown up in a parenting culture where saying "Good job!" seems to be some sort of unspoken requirement. There is a difference between celebrating successes with your children and automatically saying "Good job!" at every little thing they do in an attempt to "reward" them and promote a particular behavior or increase their self-esteem. We call the latter situation "sugarcoated manipulative praise," and your children do not need it. Alfie Kohn puts it this way: "When unconditional support is present, 'Good job!' isn't necessary; when it's absent, 'Good job!' won't help" (2001).

So when your child completes the puzzle, looks over at you, and says, "I did it!" allow his enjoyment to fill you up and spill out of you naturally. No need to push out a smile or a phrase. When your daughter finishes traversing a long log and is standing at the other side looking back on her path, try quietly appreciating not only her newly acquired level of balance and focus, but also her own private enjoyment in her little success. Enjoying and celebrating with your children has a different feel than pumping them up. See if you can begin to recognize the difference.

Start with Your Heart

But what about when your child acts out? Is unconditional love really the way to address his behavior then? Unconditional love will not solve all problems, but it is almost always a good place to start. So before jumping in to correct his behavior, start by feeling your child from your heart (see mindfulness awareness practice 8, in the preceding chapter). Take a breath into your heart, and feel his state register in your body. This practice settles your own nervous system into a clearer, more connected, and trustable state. It also helps your child get re-regulated, and he becomes more likely to follow your guidance. Starting by feeling from your heart is powerful because you're working *through the relationship*, rather than intimidating your child into compliance.

Sometimes, like in the example of the seven-year-old cleaning up the toys at the beginning of this chapter, choosing kindness and transmitting the love will be all that is needed to promote a respectful change in your child's behavior. At other times, further direction will be required, but this is neither a problem nor a contradiction. Having found your heart, you have skillfully laid the groundwork for a discipline moment.

Say "Yes" While Saying "No"

Your children are going to start to assert themselves. This is a natural part of their individuation. Through their behavior, they will—in part—be asking you, "Can I really be me—can I really feel and express what I feel—and still have your love?" If we want our children to become autonomous—and paradoxically if we want them to also be empathic and compassionate—we must do our best to communicate, "Yes. Absolutely. I want you to be *you*. I may have to help you with appropriate expression so you don't hurt other people or yourself, but that is a separate issue." Allow space for them to assert their will wherever appropriate. And where the behavior or the desired outcome is not appropriate, say "yes" to their inner world, and separately say "no" to the outer-world action.

Say your three-year-old son becomes frustrated because another boy has a toy that he wants, and he is about to hit the other boy. You grab his little arm as he is about to swing—communicating a clear "no" to the hitting—but get down low, use a soft, but clear voice, and make eye contact to let him know that all is well. You may say to him, "I can see you're frustrated, but we don't hit, buddy." Your nonverbal communication is saying that neither his frustration nor his behavior can disrupt your connection. The overall transmission is, "You and I are fine. It is just that behavior that doesn't work right now."

This reduces feelings of shame and frustration and will help him develop emotional intelligence and better self-control in the long run. And perhaps most importantly, your son will trust your guidance more in the future; he knows you are with him through thick and thin. When we do this well, our children will become better able to modify their behavior because they don't feel a sense of shame. Too often parents say "No!" with such a force and lack of connection that children come to think there is something wrong with them as a person. When we say "no" to the behavior, but stay connected to them and let them know through eye contact, tone of voice, and body language that "you and I are fine," they internalize the experience in a completely different way. Through repeated experiences of saying "yes" while saying "no," their implicit sense becomes, "There is nothing bad or wrong with me. I just made a mis-take and need to practice in this area more." This preserves their sense of self as a *process*, which is absolutely essential for healthy, lifelong growth.

Look Deeper than Behavior

Identifying *needs* and then taking charge of meeting those needs promotes the development of discipline far more than trying to simply punish or reward *behaviors*. Children benefit when you sense into their inner world and reflect to them that you get them. And there will be times when their *want* is not actually their *need*. Regardless of your ultimate decision, taking the time to understand where they are coming from is a very important first step.

So the next time your four-year-old pushes his little brother down, resist the initial impulse to "teach him a lesson." Instead, inquire into what his need is. Does he just really need to move his body and express himself in an energetic way right now? If so, maybe you say, "Hey buddy, come on, let's go roughhouse on the trampoline together." In this way, you meet his need rather than focusing on his "bad behavior" and adding more frustration to his situation.

Maybe he is frustrated because he is not getting enough one-on-one time with you. If you recognize this as the underlying source of his frustration, make a plan to hang out, just the two of you. In the meanwhile, you may still have to communicate to him that he can't push his little brother so hard like that. But you also understand that he is frustrated and you will help support him as best you can until you are able to meet him in his place of need. Feeling understood and not "bad," he becomes better able to respond in a more responsible and respectful way. And this helps him stretch a little, increasing his capacity for self-regulation.

Unconditional Love as Intention and Attitude

We want to make one thing crystal clear: we don't expect that you will always be in a state of unconditional love. We certainly aren't. Parenting is stressful, and we are pushed over our limit many times every day. It is helpful to have realistic expectations and to not put too much pressure on ourselves.

As we've said before, intentions are best thought of as a *direction* rather than a destination. If you find that on a particular day, despite breathing through the heart or engaging in metta practice (see mindfulness awareness practice 9, later in this chapter), you still are not feeling love, then direct your attention to what is here in this moment. Maybe as you breathe in and out of your heart you become aware of pain or frustration or numbness. This is okay. It is simply what you are feeling. From this truth of your experience, you may then discern that the next appropriate response is to bring your mindful awareness to the pain and welcome it with a kind, interested attention, asking, "What is this pain? What is it about? What is it here to teach me?" We cannot control much of how our bodies and minds react to life, but sometimes we can consciously choose what kind of support to bring to the inevitable suffering we all face.

It is extremely valuable to practice attending to our own experience in an unconditionally loving way if we are going to be able to attend to our children in kind. Mindful awareness is about attending to—actually "tending to"—our experience with care and acceptance. The acceptance stems from a recognition that what is happening *is* already happening. We may not like it or want it to be this way, but this is what is here now. Seeing the present moment with clarity and kindness sets the stage for skillful and compassionate action. This self-attunement can calm inner turbulence and enable us to better care for our children.

With unconditional love as an intention, we try to catch ourselves when we are being judgmental and pushing away the truth of our child's experience or our own. When we recognize that we are in a reactive state, we may discipline ourselves by trying out a practice like putting a space between reaction and action (which is captured in mindfulness awareness practice 10, in the next chapter). Or we simply decide to keep our mouths shut and refrain from disciplining our children until we have gotten ourselves together a little bit. Practicing moving toward unconditionality is a great opportunity for each of us to "grow up" right alongside of our children.

So more than achieving a certain state, we are suggesting you try bringing an *attitude* of kind, interested attention to whatever situation you find yourself in. When your child comes in upset from an argument she is having with a friend, a soft and open attitude will begin helping her without your saying a word. In a moment when you are feeling really guilty about being harsh with your three-year-old, a kind and gentle attitude toward yourself will begin the process of repair. The attitude of lovingkindness is a powerful container in which healing and reconnection can begin to take root.

The practice of unconditional love is not about perfectionism; it's not about right and wrong. Rather, it is an invitation to step in the direction of our common humanity and toward cultivating attitudes that support a richer experience and a more wholesome development. Rumi points to this practice when he says, "Out beyond ideas of right and wrong there is a field. I'll meet you there" (Collopy 2002, 109). In that field of humility, we find that our very nature is love.

And lastly, bringing an attitude of unconditional love to your home can make life so much more enjoyable and fulfilling. When we do things that open our hearts—watch an inspiring and heartfelt movie, read beautiful poetry, listen to powerful music, or simply feel our children from our hearts—our experience of life becomes enriched. We may find ourselves in exactly the same outer circumstance with our child, but by shifting our interior landscape to one of love, our relationship to the moment transforms its texture.

Mindfulness Awareness Practice 9:
Lovingkindness (Metta) Meditation

Begin by sitting in a comfortable position. Connect with the body and the breath, and if it is comfortable, place one hand over your heart center. If you can, feel the movement and vibration of your heart beating. Recognize that in this moment your heart is sending blood that carries oxygen and nutrients to every cell in your body. Feel how the heart is naturally taking care of you. You don't have to think about it, or do it right. You simply can rest into this natural process.

As you are ready, consciously invite in an intention for this practice; for example, "to open my heart," "to cultivate lovingkindness," "to invite self-compassion and self-kindness." Begin to send lovingkindness toward yourself. You can see if certain phrases emerge that express what you wish most deeply for yourself. These phrases are general enough that you can eventually send them to all beings. Traditional phrases include, "May I be safe. May I be happy. May I be healthy. May I live with ease. May I be free from suffering."

Gently and silently repeat these phrases on your own, wishing yourself well over and over again. Allow the phrases to flow through your being; allow your mind to rest, and your body to be at ease. When you become aware that your mind has wandered from the phrases and the present moment, gently yet firmly begin reciting the phrases again, perhaps with a little variation: "May I be safe. May I be happy. May I be healthy. May I live with ease."

If you become aware of the arising of any resistance to accepting these wishes for yourself, simply note these thoughts and feelings in the body, then gently return to the practice of repeating the phrases. Even if they feel like hollow words, simply continue with patience and kindness and observe your reactions. There is no "right" way to feel; you are simply planting the seeds of kindness. These seeds will bloom when they are ready.

For the next part of the practice, call to mind your child. If you have multiple children, go through this process for each one individually. Bringing to mind different images of your child, and feeling your deep desire for her to be safe, healthy, and happy, begin to offer the same phrases of lovingkindness to her: "May you be safe. May you be happy. May you be healthy. May you live with ease." Imagine your words traveling across space and time and being received by your child. Feel the sensations in your own heart as you continue sending your well-wishes to her.

Ultimately, our intention is to open our hearts and wish all beings well. We attempt to direct the phrases of lovingkindness to all beings everywhere, without distinction and without separation. Recognizing that just as we wish for ourselves and our children to be safe and protected, healthy and happy, so too does every human being wish for this.

All beings simply want to be safe, healthy, happy, and free. As it feels right to you, send lovingkindness to all beings everywhere: "May all beings live in safety, be happy, be healthy, live with ease, and be free from suffering."

Doing this practice at night as you lie in bed is a great way to soothe your nervous system and open your heart after a long and challenging day (Shapiro and Carlson 2009).

Summary

Unconditional love is a fundamental ingredient in creating harmony in the home while simultaneously supporting the development of self-discipline. When we as parents commit to creating periods of each day where we move out of judgmental thinking and reactivity into a more open state of acceptance and love, we set the tone for the entire household. Through our embodiment of love and openness, we draw our children toward greater cooperation and teamwork. The field of unconditional love directly supports your child's basic trust in reality and preserves her inherent sense of value. From this state of deep relaxation, we all remain more authentic, appreciative, and loving.

> How did the rose ever open its heart and give to this world all its beauty? It felt the encouragement of light against its being; otherwise we all remain too frightened.
>
> —Hafiz, "It Felt Love," *The Gift*

7.

SPACE

Supporting Autonomy, Competence, and Responsibility

We have a cultural notion that if children were not engineered, if we did not manipulate them, they would grow up as beasts in the field. This is the wildest fallacy in the world.

—Joseph Chilton Pearce (personal communication)

Despite its being fifteen degrees outside and snowing, Violet wanted to wear her bathing suit to kindergarten. Her mother Sara gave her several reasons why that would not be a good idea, but Violet was fixated on wearing the suit. Sara—well aware of the importance of giving children choice in the affairs of their lives—danced with her daughter for a while until they finally arrived at a compromise. Violet proudly paraded into school that morning wearing her two-piece bathing suit over her warm clothes. Sara's cheeks were rosy, and the social norms were a little shaken up that day. But more importantly, Violet's sense of autonomy and her connection with her mom were preserved and deepened by the simple gifts of space and sovereignty.

What Is Space?

Like all living things, children need room in order to grow. If their minds and bodies are too crowded with stimulation and information, including our ideas and perspectives, they will not become able to know—and *be*—themselves. The act of noninterference is the provision of space. We let our little one choose her outfits and explore what she is interested in. In order to live an authentic life, she needs us to provide her space so that she may reflect on what she thinks and feels, as well as find her own heartfelt motivations for respectful and responsible living.

Children also need room to continue developing their own internal "gyroscope of natural self-regulation" (Kohn 2005, 58). If we focus on controlling them rather than giving them space to learn and practice steering their own ship, it will stunt their development toward healthy self-discipline. When you begin to understand the value of space in your child's development, you will intuitively find ways to provide this form of nourishment. And perhaps more importantly, when you begin to *experience* a sense of spaciousness you will not only find yourself reacting and controlling less, but also enjoying the moments with your children more.

How Space Nourishes

The element of space supports aspects of a child's development that can be described as feelings of autonomy, the development of competence, and a sense of responsibility for one's actions. These in turn support the development of the child's compassion and her healthy self-discipline. Space nourishes through its implicit nod of confidence to the child and to her inherent and emerging capacities.

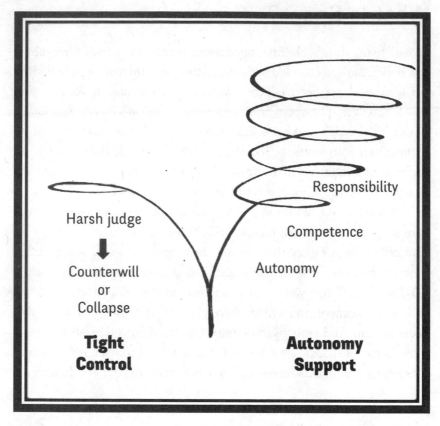

Figure 6: The Fruits of Autonomy Support

Autonomy and Competence

Children are born with a desire to be autonomous, to steer their own ship, and to become more and more competent in the ways of the world. They have a natural curiosity and interest in how the world works. They enjoy wrestling with problems, coming up with solutions, and testing out their theories. And yet these qualities, natural to childhood, too frequently become lost somewhere along the way to adulthood. Much of the loss is caused by excessive manipulation and unnecessary pressure from adults (Kohn 2005). When we give our children room to experiment, problem solve, and learn from these encounters, they remain curious and grow more autonomous and capable over time. This is the natural arc of human development if we can temper our impulse to meddle.

Responsibility

When we allow our children to feel some degree of autonomy and control over their lives, they grow up feeling like they are in the driver's seat of their lives. This is what psychologists refer to as a *sense of agency*. This is the opposite of a *victim mentality*, which develops when a child is subjected to excessive control. When their autonomy and sense of agency are preserved, children begin to feel responsible for their actions. They then take more ownership over the decisions they make and pay better attention to the consequences of their choices (Neufeld and Maté 2004).

It is important that our children retain their self-motivation and sense they have some power over their lives, not only for the sake of their own development but also for greater harmony in our homes. When children experience a sense of autonomy and sovereignty over their lives they act out less, and have a stronger desire to cooperate and be a team player.

As Dr. Pearce points out in this chapter's opening quote, our culture has a strong bias that children need to be trained in order to behave. In particular, the authoritarian view of children is that they are inherently bad and they need to be punished and rewarded in order to make them good. And while it is plain that children are fairly self-centered and have poor impulse control for the first years of their lives, current research argues against this notion of children as "bad." Alfie Kohn, after analyzing dozens of studies on children and empathy, notes that young children are equally as likely to be empathic and cooperative as they are to be selfish (2005). Further, the controlling methods of punishment and reward do not make people more empathic and ethical; they make them less so (Cotton 1995).

A key effect of supporting a child's autonomy is that it preserves his *desire* to be responsible, kind, and compassionate. If a child's experience is that he is forced to be generous and share, he will be disconnected from his natural desire to do so. If being connected to people includes respect for his own autonomy, then he will find ways to act in harmony with those around him. The nourishing aspects of relationship will draw out his authentic motivation to be kind and compassionate. To paraphrase Alfie Kohn, it's not the amount of motivation that counts—it's the type (2005). A life motivated by love is healthier, more attuned, and more sustainable than a life driven by fear.

Autonomy Support versus Tight Control

So what kinds of interactions will support our child in developing into an autonomous being who remains engaged in ongoing social and emotional learning? The research is clear that if you want your child to develop healthy self-discipline, *autonomy support* is a better long-term strategy than *tight control* (Grolnick 2009). Supporting autonomy means helping your child feel that he has some measure of choice and control over the events of his life: if not over the *what*, at least over *when*, *where*, and *how* to do the things you need him to do. Children who receive more support of their autonomy from the adults in their lives get better grades, develop greater conceptual understanding of whatever they are learning, exhibit enhanced persistence in school and sports, are more productive, display less burnout, and have greater levels of psychological well-being. In essence, they feel better and function better in the many domains of their lives. And why? Because their own authentic motivation has been preserved. Using strategies that promote autonomy support, you help your child grow into an independent young adult capable of pursuing his own version of success.

On the other hand, tight control fails to support the skills necessary for long-term success. The pressure of punishments and rewards can lead to short-term changes in behavior, but rarely perserves those changed behaviors later on in life, when no one is around to entice us with a carrot or threaten us with a stick (Kohn 2005). Punishments and rewards activate primitive circuits in our limbic systems and midbrains and leave memory traces about what causes us pain and what brings us pleasure.

The problem is that the more we use these circuits to train our child, the less the circuits of authentic motivation and empathy are being used and strengthened. Over time children who are "trained" lack development of their own internal moral compass. In short, tight control will not help strengthen the neural pathways needed for true empathy, responsibility, and ethical behavior. Tight control is a short-term strategy focused on compliance at the expense of the self-motivation needed to do the right thing in a sustained and healthy way.

In his groundbreaking book *Drive*, Daniel Pink summarizes the research on the effects of rewards and punishments to motivate people (2009). Here are what he calls "the seven deadly flaws of carrots and sticks":

1. They diminish performance (except on simple, repetitive tasks).

2. They crush creativity.

3. They crowd out good behavior.

4. They foster short-term thinking.

5. They encourage shortcuts, cheating, and unethical behavior.

6. They become addictive.

7. They extinguish intrinsic motivation (one's own *authentic* desire to do the right thing).

One quick look at this list should give us pause, especially the part about extinguishing intrinsic (authentic) motivation. As Pink puts it, "Control leads to compliance; autonomy leads to engagement" (2009, 108).

Recall that self-discipline generally evolves through three stages: the impulsive self, the judge, and the authentic self. If we use carrots and sticks as a *primary* means to get our child to behave, his development tends to stall out at the level of the judge. And because of constant manipulation, these children tend to spend more time in the survival mode, creating a combination of harsh judgment and reactivity. Behavior held in check primarily by a harsh judge is less sustainable, less flexible, less attuned to others and to the needs of the moment, and has greater costs to our health and well-being. Let's take a look at how this comes about.

Counterwill

Tight control leads to chronic use of two protective instincts hard-wired into our brains: counterwill and collapse. *Counterwill* is a term used by Gordon Neufeld and Gabor Maté to describe the instinct to push back when we are feeling controlled or disrespected (2004). When your five-year-old feels his autonomy is being threatened, you might hear "NO!" or "You're not the boss of me!" This is simply a protective reaction designed to preserve his sense of sovereignty over his life. This reaction—although not always fun for us as parents—is a healthy sign that he is protective of his own right to exist and to have some measure of choice in his life. This instinct is designed to protect him while he is still developing his own center of authentic motivation.

As parents, we need to find our way in the dance between giving him autonomy and helping him develop a healthy respect for authority. If we control him too much, he may become stuck in a chronic state of counterwill, pushing back against everyone and everything just to feel some sense of autonomy over his life. On the other hand, if we let him climb into the alpha position too much, he is likely to become more anxious and controlling over time. Recall that children come to a state of rest when they are lovingly invited to depend on us for protection, care, and guidance until they are capable of providing for themselves. If we allow the natural developmental plan to become inverted—allow our child to become the alpha—the result is that fear and reactivity will become his predominant state (Neufeld and Maté 2004). The dance is to feel which is needed in any given moment while remaining the ultimate authority. Ask yourself, "Which form of nourishment will bring him to a state of rest—*space* to experience autonomy, or a *firm boundary* to help him adapt to the realities of the situation?" To grow up whole, he needs both.

Collapse

The other instinctual reaction to tight control is *collapse*. Some children more than others will react to pressure and coercion by collapsing into the will of the "boss." A child's emotional brain may feel that it is either too dangerous to push back or that her resistance will threaten her connection to her parent. As a result, she submits in order to avoid a confrontation and the loss of connection. This may seem desirable on the surface. You wanted her to clean up her toys, you threatened her with a punishment, and she got the message and complied with your demand. What is wrong with that? The problems are fourfold.

First, you are heading down the path of creating a victim mentality; you are teaching her that it is hopeless to resist, and so giving in becomes her practiced response to life. The more a child is controlled by her parents, the more this becomes her pattern. This leaves her more susceptible to being used and abused by others. Second, since she does not feel like she's at the steering wheel of her life, she does not feel a sense of responsibility for her actions. She is less likely to take initiative and problem solve on her own. Third, she has not had the space to feel into her own authentic motivations, and has a harder time knowing what she really wants and needs. Her authenticity and self-expression suffer as a result. Fourth—and perhaps most important—too much pressure and coercion ruins your relationship with her. A child in a tightly controlled environment does not receive the attunement and space needed to deepen into a safe, loving relationship. Instead she receives the message that the rules are more important to her parents than her own dignity and happiness. You have to ask yourself if the downsides of a victim mentality—irresponsibility, inauthenticity, and decreased connection with your child—are worth the short-term gains achieved through punishments and rewards.

Now, to be clear, occasional use of consequences for inappropriate behavior, or of treats for good behavior, will not do permanent damage to your child. We all experience positive and negative consequences as a result of our behavior everyday. Rewards and punishments are part of daily life, and we have brain circuits specifically designed to remember these outcomes. But research tells us that when used as a *primary* means of teaching our children how to behave, carrots and sticks do not support the development of one's authentic source of respectful and responsible behaviors. We will address the healthy use of firm and clear boundaries and occasional consequences in chapter ten.

Space in Everyday Life

Since giving children space helps them feel a greater sense of autonomy, responsibility, and desire to become more competent and connected to others, it can be helpful to aim to provide the nourishment of space everyday. There are plenty of opportunities. In some moments, it can be as easy as a lack of interference with their flow.

One way we can do this is by making the intention to not interfere unless it is really necessary. This is an especially worthwhile strategy when you are in a reactive state, and your interventions are thus more likely to come out of your own emotional charge than an attunement to what your child actually needs. This intention is a capacity we can practice and build within ourselves; the following mindfulness awareness practice, which only takes a minute, can help build this skill. The practice is especially helpful for those of us who tend to be more controlling.

Mindfulness Awareness Practice 10:
Putting a Space Between Reaction and Action

The next time it feels as though your child needs a response from you, consider pausing first before you react. Become aware of your body and internal state by taking a few breaths and sensing yourself. Before engaging in a knee-jerk reaction, count at least one breath, in and out. This will allow for conscious responding instead of automatic reacting. Once you have taken a full breath, then you can move to stabilize the tower he is building (if it really needs it); or say, "I really like that drawing"; or open into a smile: whatever action feels right given the context of the situation. Often, nothing really needs to be done, and the pause will help you realize this, allowing you and your child to simply rest into spacious being. The point here is to create more space from our habitual reactions and to allow (perhaps) a more authentic response to emerge.

Inserting a space between your inner reaction and your outer action is not only healthy for your child, but also allows you to sit back, rest, and enjoy life a little more. Parenting is a really demanding job, but sometimes we put in more effort than we need to.

Protection

A good place to start when moving toward providing space is to create a certain amount of healthy protection. You may, for example, childproof the house so your toddler can explore free from a thousand "no"s a day. You may set up periods of the day when the house is a quiet zone for reading, creative projects, or rest. And you may limit the more intense forms of media exposure so your child's mind does not become preoccupied with scary thoughts and images. Once you feel the value of spaciousness, you will intuitively come up with ways to provide it.

Support Autonomy, Competence, and Responsibility

Let your four-year-old pour her own milk. Sure, she'll spill some now and again; we all do. But she will get better at it the more she practices. You can help scaffold her emerging capacities by holding the glass steady at first, if she is okay with it; but try not to completely take over. What is most important is that she feels your confidence in her through the fact that you are giving her some autonomy and space.

And when she spills some milk, no need to make a big deal of it. Just point to the rag and let her take care of her mess. She will feel better about you not being upset with her and feel more competent to do the whole thing herself. She will also pay more attention to pouring with a steady hand in the future, knowing that any cleanup will be her responsibility. This approach also lessens our frustration. Many times we end up acting like a martyr, feeling like it is always up to us to clean up the messes, and therefore we get more controlling, trying to prevent further work for ourselves. Inherent in our children's development is a deepening desire for initiative and self-responsibility. So share the workload and invite your daughter into her natural desire to help.

Micromanage Less

When we give our children the leadership role from time to time, they come to feel a greater sense of power, freedom, and responsibility. Let her choose her clothes and put them on herself. Let her know that the mess needs to be cleaned up and then give her the space to figure out how. Be available as a resource, but let her manage the project to the degree she is able.

Boundaries are often necessary, but they are more effective if we keep them wide and subtle. Recognize where you have the power and where you don't. Otherwise you will reveal your impotence and possibly become frustrated and aggressive. For example, don't try to force your child to eat her food. Offer tasty and nutritious meals, and sit back and let her decide if she wants to eat or not. You can let her know, "This is what we are having tonight, sweetheart. Nothing else once the table is cleared." But then let it go and enjoy each other; don't make it an issue. (I [Chris] have been a pediatrician for fifteen years and can assure you: children don't starve themselves from a place of choice.)

Or, when you want your four-year-old to get his pajamas on before watching the *Dora the Explorer* video you promised him, don't start by pushing the boundary in his face. A tight control method would be to say, "Put your pajamas on now or you cannot watch your video." Can you sense the immediate pressure he probably feels? The consequence is delivered as a threat and is likely to provoke feelings of frustration, hurt, and resistance.

Instead try, "Hey Cody, can you go get your pajamas on?" and let it rest for a minute or two while he becomes sidetracked. He comes over and says, "I am ready for my movie now." And then you say, "Oh, I'm happy to turn on your movie once your pajamas are on." The parameters are clear: the pajamas need to be on before the movie starts. And most importantly, Cody can make that happen. You have given him a measure of autonomy and control. You are not starting by threatening him. The place where you have the power is in turning on the movie or not, and you rest comfortably knowing this and allowing him the room he needs to step into his "yes" or his "no." He has the freedom to choose "pajamas and a movie" or "no pajamas and no movie." This is how you set a boundary yet provide autonomy support.

Try for "Win-Wins"

Be on the lookout for "limits for limits' sake"—for the sake of *control* only. Too many of these kinds of limits will end up backfiring on you. Instead, clearly state your "bottom line"—what you are really worried about—and then invite your child to find a way to solve the problem and meet both of your needs. Instead of telling your eight-year-old, "You cannot go to the park alone with your friend," explain your concerns to him. Let him know that you are worried about the busy road bordering the park. He may then offer a plan: "How about you walk us over there, and we promise to stay in the playground away from the road? And then you come and get us to cross back in one hour?" If that adequately addresses your concerns, you have helped support a "win-win."

When the true contours of your boundary are communicated respectfully rather than in absolute terms, your children feel your desire for them to be safe and happy. They know you are looking out for them. And they feel respected, having been given a chance to negotiate and problem solve with you. You do, of course, have the ultimate say. But save it for when it is really necessary.

Support Grit and Resilience

Many children these days have been robbed of the value of struggle. Too often, we parents jump in at the slightest sign of frustration to help our children. But there is great value in persisting in the face of difficulty—what is often called *grit*: perseverance and passion for long-term goals (Pink 2009). Challenge puts pressure on our creative brain to come up with solutions. Difficulties exercise the prefrontal cortex as a child must try to stay focused and regulated despite increasing frustration. This "frustration" is simply the energy that his brain generates to help him get to a goal. Frustration is not something to always be stamped out or avoided; rather, it is important for our sons and daughters to learn to work with it. Learning how to handle frustration and other difficult emotions is crucial for the development of self-regulation and resilience. As Viktor Frankl wrote, "What man actually needs is not a tensionless state but rather the striving and struggling for a worthwhile goal, a freely chosen task" (1992, 110).

So let your three-year-old struggle sometimes with getting the seat buckle snapped in place. Some days you will do it for him; other days you will stabilize the buckle while he snaps it in. And on a few days, let him struggle with it and actually experience frustration. Express a steady confidence in him and his abilities. You are helping him build an important life skill and a sense of capacity around being able to persist in the face of challenges.

Space as Intention and Attitude

By setting an intention for spaciousness, we try to protect our children from too much stimulation and intrusion, and support their quiet contact with themselves. But despite our best intentions, family life will still frequently be hectic. What can we do? We suggest trying to bring an *attitude* of spaciousness to the turmoil itself. Instead of getting all caught up in the craziness, try giving the maelstrom all the room it needs to be just as it is. No need to control it; open *beyond* it.

The following mindfulness awareness practice can help you learn to do this. By practicing feeling spacious, we begin to trust life more, trust ourselves more, and trust our children more. We begin to recognize that it is not all up to us, but that there is a dynamic, self-organizing intelligence inside of every living thing. We begin to sense the support all around us more than our fears and our need to control. When we can relax into the felt sense of this truth everything unfolds more easefully.

Mindfulness Awareness Practice 11:
Getting Spacious

Do this practice the first time when you are alone or do not have to interact with anybody. Begin by sitting in a comfortable posture where you can take a deep breath. Inhale deeply, becoming aware of the in-breath filling your belly and then your chest. Exhale and feel the breath leaving your body and emptying out and filling the space around you. On the next inhale, really feel the breath expanding the space in your belly and chest, and on the exhale, visualize that air spreading out from your body in all directions: out the front, out the back, to the left, to the right, above your head, and down around your legs and feet. As you breathe out, allow your awareness to spread out into the space, forming a bubble a few feet out from your body in all directions. *Feel* the space around you. Continue to repeat this cycle: inhale and fill the belly and chest, then exhale and relax outward in all directions, allowing any tension you have in your body or mind to dissolve outward into the room. If it feels right, you can allow the bubble to expand over time to fill the entire room or area where you are practicing.

With practice, you will be able to "get spacious" right in the middle of a meltdown, or your children fighting over a toy. Allow the tension and desire for control to arise, and then dissolve outwards beyond this small sense of self and become more spacious and loving in the process. Life will continue to be crazy; the waves of chaos do not cease. But our relationship to the chaos can evolve with moments of intentional practice.

In her diary, Anne Frank wrote, "How true Daddy's words were when he said: 'All children must look after their own upbringing.' Parents can only give good advice or put them on the right paths, but the final forming of a person's character lies in their own hands" (1952, 206). When we take time to get spacious, this truth becomes self-evident, and informs our parenting for the better.

Summary

Authoritative parenting methods of autonomy support—of creating space to allow our child's inherent developmental unfolding—have clear benefits over authoritarian methods of manipulation and control. Through cultivating spaciousness in our parenting and in our relationship with our children, we begin to soften the impulses of our need to control. The fruit of our practice will be children who are self-motivated, self-directed, and capable of respectful and responsible behaviors when we are not around to police them. In this way, we will increasingly be able to let go of the reins and enjoy watching our children be, and become, fully themselves.

> [Once] the realization is accepted that even between
> the closest human beings infinite distances continue
> to exist, a wonderful living side by side can grow up,
> if they succeed in loving the distance between them,
> which makes it possible for each to see the other
> whole and against a wide sky!

—Rainer Maria Rilke, "Letter to Emanuel von Bodman"

8.

MENTORSHIP

Promoting Healthy Habits, Strong Values, and Emotional Intelligence

For only as we ourselves, as adults, actually move and have our being in the state of love, can we be appropriate models and guides for our children. What we are teaches the child far more than what we say, so we must be what we want our children to become.

—Joseph Chilton Pearce (personal communication)

One summer day, on a dare, Carl knocked over a neighbor's mailbox when he thought no one was watching. He was seen and his dad received a call. "Go to the shed and get out our work gloves and a shovel, and then meet me out front," his dad said firmly. Carl went straight to the shed, his heart pounding. His friend Greg had recently received a public shaming from his dad for a similar act. Carl was really scared.

At the neighbor's house, Carl's dad offered a very heartfelt apology and turned to Carl: "Your turn." Heart racing and flushed with embarrassment, Carl stepped up to look his victim in the eye, and gave his best version of an apology.

Carl and his dad spent the rest of the day repairing the mailbox. Dad had Carl do most of the work, providing occasional tactical support, but mostly staying quiet and solemn. Dad had to repeatedly resist his impulse to scold Carl—to teach him a lesson. He was angry and embarrassed, but he intuited that silence would be more powerful than aggression. When they were finished, Dad asked, "Does this make it right?" Carl reflected for a moment, went to the house alone, and offered an afternoon of his time to help the neighbor with yard work or any project he needed help with.

Later that night, after a quiet dinner, Carl's dad came into his room. He sat down on the bed and told Carl about a time he had destroyed a boy's fort "for fun." He spoke of how ashamed he felt when he had to "fess up" to what he had done in his moment of impulsiveness, and how he had to watch the boy cry in his mother's arms. Dad's story and vulnerability impacted Carl visibly, and Dad moved in close to put an arm around him. It was a tender moment filled with sadness and regret, but also closeness and a measure of growing up.

What Is Mentorship?

One of the most important dimensions of parenting is being a guide and a mentor to your children. The Oxford English Dictionary defines *mentor* as "an experienced and trusted advisor" (2nd ed., s.v. "mentor"). Notice that *trust* is a key part of the mentoring relationship. It is not just our knowledge and experience that matter, but especially that our children *trust us* to guide them through turbulent and uncertain times.

As we mentioned earlier, mentorship is a yang element: we are purposely trying to shape the contours of our home or our child's behavioral expressions. The yin elements of unconditional love and space serve to create a deep well of trust, connection, and respect between us and our children. This makes it possible to guide our children when necessary. Through the gift of mentorship we can organize the flow of our homes and draw out the natural heartfelt potentials of our children.

It is important to remember that mentorship is not primarily a downloading of information and values into our children. Yes, learning is part of the picture. But there is no amount of teaching that can replace the power of human development and maturity. Self-discipline, emotional intelligence, and resilience are indispensable capacities, and they are not taught; they are grown.

Lastly, mentorship is not a one-way street. Becoming a mentor worth trusting means that we as parents need to continue growing up as well. Parenthood is a place where we are stretched beyond our selfishness into a wider version of who and what we are. It seems that life's plan is to use this great and beautiful occasion to further our development and enrich our world. Michael Meade puts it this way: "Mentoring keeps a culture vital in two ways: by encouraging the great gifts and innovative contributions of its young people, and by giving adults an opportunity to grow into the role of guiding elders" (Meade, Some, Rodriguez, Kornfield, and Bishop, n.d.).

How Mentorship Nourishes

Mentorship nourishes our children through a range of mechanisms, from modeling to consultation to direct guidance. In the early years, our mentorship serves to create healthy habits and helps us pass down our most heartfelt values as well as our knowledge and know-how. But increasingly over the years—and building on this foundation—we hope that our children begin to develop their own emotional understanding of the value of responsible and respectful behavior. If you do your job well, emotional intelligence will grow, giving your child the moral compass she needs to live her life with compassion, authenticity, and integrity (see figure 7).

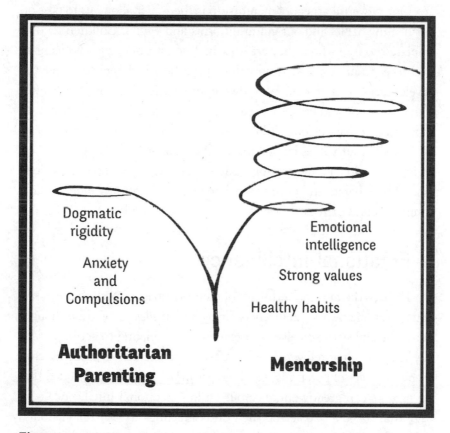

Figure 7: The Fruits of Mentorship

Children need some degree of direction and guidance because they are new to the world and have a lot to learn. Nature has provided a natural period of dependency upon caregivers. There are plenty of things we can teach our children about the world and how it works—we show them how to tie their shoes, how to put together a meal, and how to approach organizing a work project. Sometimes it is good for children to learn things on their own (space); other times it is helpful to have some guidance (mentorship).

Healthy Habits and Values

One powerful aspect of mentorship is the way it allows us to pass on our healthy habits and our cultural norms and values. Children tend to emulate those to whom they are attached, so part of our job is to create structures, routines, and rituals that serve health, happiness, and the development of character. When we consistently wash our hands after using the potty, and brush our teeth together before bed, these activities soon become part of our child's habitual, health-promoting repertoire. He absorbs your values by hearing you say "please" and "thank you," or seeing you help a mom carrying a baby or give your seat up to an elderly man. These habits and norms translate into his becoming more socially competent and increase his sense of connection to others.

Emotional Intelligence

Perhaps the most powerful gift of mentorship is supporting the development of emotional intelligence. *Emotional intelligence* can be thought of as "the ability to perceive and regulate emotion, and to act in personally and socially intelligent ways." After three decades of studying children and styles of parenting, psychologist John Gottman concluded that we parents can greatly enhance our child's emotional intelligence—an "'IQ' that is about people and the world of feelings" (1997, 17). He found that children who grow up in homes where the parents actively support emotional intelligence have more focused attention, better self-regulation, fewer behavioral problems, better social skills, better academic performance, and fewer illnesses, and are more resilient in the face of adversity (Gottman 1997). Becoming "emotional coaches" to our children empowers them in harnessing the intelligence of their social-emotional brains, and gives them a greater advantage in school, relationships, and all areas of life.

But it is essential that we don't conceptualize emotional intelligence as something that is primarily *taught*. Emotional intelligence is a natural human birthright that is *grown* over many years (Neufeld and Maté 2004). There are ways we can support emotional intelligence, but we must see our role clearly: we parents are nourishing a natural developmental process. With this orientation in mind, let's look at how we can do so optimally.

Emotional intelligence involves three interwoven aspects: *recognition, regulation,* and *appropriate expression*. Our first task as loving parents is to recognize emotions—in ourselves and in our children. We then modulate the flow of emotion into an optimal range, helping to temper too-intense emotions while not squashing the emotions completely. And lastly, we move toward appropriate expression of emotion, which includes setting boundaries on actions that are harmful. Over time, these aspects of emotional intelligence that we model become the habits and capacities of our children.

Emotional intelligence supports your child in acting in increasingly wise and compassionate ways. He comes to know his inner world of motivations and feelings with clarity. He knows when to stay steadfast and focused, and when to rest. He becomes more attuned to others, better able to empathize and act with a more heartfelt conscience. Emotional intelligence becomes his compass and self-discipline his ship on the journey into adulthood.

Mentorship in Everyday Life

There are so many things in daily life that we can teach our children. We can show a child how animals like to be petted and how to avoid being bitten. We can teach him about emotions—how to identify them and work with them in constructive rather than destructive ways. We can show him how to make a schedule or a chart to help keep him on track toward his goals and aspirations. We can save him from having to reinvent the wheel by passing on what we have learned.

But we will be more effective in the long run if we try to become *learning companions* more than teachers (Gamper 2011). The goal of a learning companion is to facilitate the child in his process of discovery and learning, rather than seeing him as a receptacle in which to pour information and knowledge. A learning companion recognizes when the child is fully focused and engrossed in what he is doing. Psychologists call this experience *flow*, and it is essential for mental health and well-being (Pink 2009). The good news is that you don't need to know how to create this experience, only how to recognize it and not interfere.

So let your toddler continue to collect water from the bucket, pour it into his pitcher, and then water the bush over and over again. His enjoyment naturally organizes his focus, strengthens his hand-eye coordination, and will expand his project-management skills. When your nine-year-old is working hard on getting his bike back together, spare him your daddy-wisdom and let his absorption in the project inform him about the mechanics. Some things are best learned without a teacher.

A learning companion also often asks more questions than gives answers. For young children, "You need to clean up your mess" can become "What do we need to do before we can have our snack?" The children pause, reflect, remember, and engage in the cleanup. It often feels better to be asked than to be told what to do.

If your child says he wants to build a birdhouse, you could simply outline the steps that need to happen to prepare to start the project. But alternatively, you could ask him a series of questions, like "Okay, what materials do you think we will need? What tools? Where do you think we should set up to do the project?" In this way, he becomes actively engaged in thinking about the project and planning. The project really becomes his—he has much more buy-in, which will naturally increase his focus and follow-through.

We can also use questions to precipitate our child's growing emotional intelligence. Once, the four-year-old son of a friend of mine (Chris's) snatched something out of Kai's hands while he was playing with it. Kai was understandably upset. But my friend did not tell her son, "That was wrong," or "Don't ever do that again," nor did she give him a time-out. Instead she bent down beside him and said, "Taj, how do you think that would feel if Kai took something out of your hands?" Taj thought for a second and then said, "Not good." And without further prompting, he went over and handed the toy back to Kai. "Thanks, sweetheart," she said, and gave him a little kiss on the head. Not only did she not make him feel bad about what he did, she precipitated his own insight and empathy. She took time to water the seeds of his emerging emotional intelligence, which will one day guide him through his life in a wise and compassionate way. We don't always have time or the patience to do it this way. But it is part of our job as parents to teach our children by drawing out their own intelligence in addition to setting boundaries in a more matter-of-fact way.

Perhaps the most powerful way we can help teach our children is through modeling. When your child is properly attached to you, she will mimic many of your behaviors. The power of imitation draws children into all kinds of behaviors from learning language to using the potty to vacuuming the floors. Young children want to be like their mommies and daddies. Doing what their parents do and acting like them helps our children feel close to us. Remembering that your children are watching and will emulate you, it can be helpful to ask yourself, "What kind of attitude do I want to bring to my yard work today? How do I want to speak to my partner? How do I model dealing with frustration and disappointment?" It's a truism that children often do not do what their parents *tell* them to do, but they rarely fail to imitate them. This can deeply motivate us to do our best every day and live our lives with grace.

Structures, Routines, and Rituals

There are many ways we can guide both our children and the flow of our homes toward harmony and ease. Perhaps one of the most important ways is through the creation of healthy structures, routines, and rituals. The banks of the river are necessary for flow to occur. When we provide routines and rituals—wake-up cuddle time, preparing the dinner table, and the wind-down, bedtime routine—children come to know what to expect, and can relax and enjoy the flow that the structures provide. The consistency provides them with a greater sense of competence and control, and lessens our workload as well.

Reduce the Morning Madness

Mornings are sometimes the most frustrating part of family life. Anything we can do to increase flow in the morning hours and get everyone out the door on time without a fight is worth the front-end work. So have your children set their clothes out the night before. Have a set wake-up time that gives everyone enough space to have breakfast, pack up, and leave on time. Set a timer or ring a bell that marks the transitions clearly. Set the timer to ring for departure: "Final pack up, shoes on, we'll leave together in five." Set your "leave-time" with a ten-minute buffer so that any untimeliness can be dealt with compassionately. If the flow is not working, have a family meeting and discuss the issue. Get the children involved, allowing them to create reasonable solutions and agree upon consequences for missing the mark. Having everyone's input will increase buy-in and cooperation.

Set the Table

One useful way to create flow is to have an agreed-upon routine for setting the dinner table. The older child can be responsible for pouring the drinks and lighting the candle, while younger children can do simpler tasks like plates, silverware, and napkins. Get everyone who is capable involved rather than doing it all yourself. You can agree on the division of labor and specifics at a family meeting, and may have to reiterate the agreement while getting the routine established. But once everyone is on board, the mealtimes will go much more smoothly because you won't have to orchestrate everyone.

Make Chores into Connecting Rituals

One of the things that many children are missing out on today is the value of meaningful work. As soon as they are able, children can be invited to participate in the creation and maintenance of beauty in their home. Pick a day of the week to do the things that need to be done, clean and straighten with pride, and instill these values in your children. Give them age-appropriate tasks and work right alongside each other. Let the preschoolers vacuum or pick up toys and put them away. Give your eight-year-old a whole project he can manage on his own, perhaps cleaning and straightening the toolshed. Turn on some music. Dance and play together. We can turn "chores" into beautifying rituals and times of togetherness.

Encourage Manners

Common decency and manners are another way we can mentor our children. Manners do not have to be some worn-out holdover from the Victorian era. The deeper purpose of manners is to open the heart and increase the flow of love and kindness. When my (Chris's) son Kai was about two, he would sometimes shout out at me in the usual, impulsive toddler way, "Daddy, I want juice!" I would then say to him in my best little-Kai voice, "Daddy, juice please!" and then I would turn to get the juice, not needing anything in return to get my little boy his drink. About half of the time, he would repeat back to me, "Daddy, juice please!" And I would say, "Of course, sweetheart. Here you go." And we would toast. By three or so, he was saying "please" unsolicited over half the time.

The purpose is not to have a well-behaved child we can brag about, but rather to promote ways of speaking and being with each other that open the heart. When our children ask sweetly, we *want* to go the extra mile for them. We want to serve them and take care of them in any way we can while they will still let us. The "pleases" and "thank yous" are meant to shift the states of the people giving and receiving them. Simple rituals, powerful effects.

Model Gratitude and Appreciation

Take each others' hands and give thanks at each mealtime for whatever you are grateful for. This connects you, opens your heart, and deepens your contact with the wider web of life. Take time to appreciate the simple pleasures, the ways that you are fortunate. Being only thirty minutes away, we get to go to the beach regularly. But I (Chris) try to remember at the end of each fantastic beach day to turn toward the ocean and the setting sun and give thanks, and feel how lucky we are to have access to such beauty and fun. The other day as we were leaving, Kai stopped and yelled out—"Wait! We didn't say good-bye and thank you to the ocean!" We all stopped and turned around to give thanks. Bodhi blew kisses and Kai said, "Thanks, ocean. We will miss you!" Hand in hand, we all took a moment to let the appreciation sink in. For me, I felt especially appreciative that this was becoming a "habit of the heart" for my boys.

The Reality Principle

Another way that mentorship nourishes our children is by helping them increasingly gain a more realistic perspective of life. We help them learn about cause and effect. We help temper their misplaced feelings of inferiority as well as their grandiosity. It is crucial we help them come to see themselves accurately: what they are capable of, what they are not, and what they still have to learn and practice if they are to succeed. We aim for a true *humility*, which connotes "being restored to the ground of your being." True confidence comes from knowing your strengths and weaknesses: when you can handle a situation on your own and when you need to ask for help (Young-Eisendrath 2008).

Sometimes we treat our children like they are made of glass, feeling that we have to always use a soft, sweet voice so as to avoid traumatizing them. This actually communicates to them, "You can't handle upsets. You are fragile and need to be always treated delicately." As a result of this message, they can become less resilient and more prone to being traumatized by the bumps and bruises of everyday life.

So, you can speak to them in a more matter-of-fact tone if that feels right to you. Because they already experience plenty of unconditional love and space, such guidance won't feel like a comment on them as a person. You might say, "That doesn't work here, buddy. Try something else." When the child succeeds in finding a socially acceptable solution, he will feel more competent and confident in his abilities.

Emotional Coaching

Supporting emotional intelligence in our children is a huge topic on which whole books are written. Here, we will simply provide a basic overview of emotional coaching, and refer you to the "suggested readings" section if you want to explore it more in depth. Let's start with a story that captures how emotional coaching might look in real life.

Your ten-year-old child comes home from school and slams the front door shut hard enough to make a picture fall off the wall and shatter on the floor. You immediately feel hot and angry and are about to yell, when you stop yourself and take a deep breath before doing anything. "Hey, buddy," you say as he is walking away. "Hold on."

He turns, scowling, and meets your gaze with steely eyes. You feel a little irritated, thinking, "Don't look at me like that. I didn't do anything to you." But you recognize he is angry and sense that something must have happened. Most importantly, you know he needs you right now. Choosing not to focus on his "bad behavior," you ask, "What's up, buddy? What's going on?" and you continue to breathe and calm yourself. He replies coldly: "Nothing." Meeting his eyes and softening your body a little bit you say, "You seem really angry about something."

"Yeah, I am angry about something!" he yells, and starts off on a rant about an incident he had at school with his friend today. You listen closely, totally attentive to what he is saying—both verbally and nonverbally. You ride the emotional waves with him as he spews the details of the story. You communicate understanding through nods and subtle vocalizations that let him know you really get where he is coming from, that you are with him. Several times during the conversation you feel the impulse to calm him down, and to give some advice about what to do.

But you patiently hear him out, staying fully present for him, and delaying moving toward a solution before it is time.

Eventually, he starts to settle down a little bit. During a span of silence, you ask a clarifying question, listen to his response, and empathize with him: "Yeah, I get it." Then you ask another. Over the next ten minutes, through your curiosity and confidence in him, you dance together toward some next steps that he might take with his friend. The conversation ends with an action plan in place, a long hug, and a feeling of closeness between the two of you. You recognize that the situation could have ended much worse, and feel blessed to have had the capacity to ride out the storm with grace and skill.

One of the keys to becoming an effective emotional coach is to begin to see your child's expressions of emotion—especially the uncomfortable, upsetting, or irritating ones—as opportunities instead of problems to be solved. All emotions are information. When we are not overwhelmed by them, emotions can teach us. They help expand our contact with the world and deepen intimacy with our loved ones. Changing the way we relate to emotion can transform our lives.

If we are to help our children regulate their emotions, we must first increase our capacity to *recognize* emotions, in ourselves as well as in our children. Emotional recognition starts with the ability to directly feel emotion through the body. We sense our feeling states—and the states of others—through our bodies. This is why we have included mindfulness awareness practices in this book, such as the body scan in chapter four and feeling from the heart in chapter five. Doing practices like these will increase your capacity for self-insight, empathy, and self-regulation, which in turn will help you guide your child through the same territory.

Simply recognizing an emotion begins the process of *regulating* it. When we are able to match a word to our primary feeling—"I am feeling *anger*"—this alone helps us regulate the intensity of the emotion; it helps us feel a degree of understanding and control. In turn, we can help our children "name it to tame it" by providing an emotional vocabulary to help them identify what they are feeling (Siegel and Bryson 2011). This will increase their ability to identify and regulate emotions in the future.

But beyond the words, simply being attuned to your child—being fully present with him and what he is going through—is profoundly soothing to his system. We can handle all manner of difficulties when we are seen, heard, and held in the midst of these emotional storms.

In addition to naming emotions, it can be helpful for us as parents to engage in practices that help modulate the intensity of what we are experiencing in the midst of emotional tempests. This is the "putting on our own oxygen mask first" approach. Mindfulness awareness practices like getting spacious (in chapter seven) or grounding down (described later in this chapter) can help shift the energy running through your body and brain and actually change the outcome of what might otherwise be an explosive and dysregulating exchange. When we become steady and present in emotional times, our nonverbal signals communicate, "Don't you worry; we'll get through this. Take all the space you need to feel what you feel. I can navigate us through this storm."

And yet allowing emotions to be fully experienced does not mean that we condone children discharging their intensity in hurtful ways. We still help them find an *appropriate response*. Often the first appropriate thing to do is help the emotion find a pathway that leads the child to greater integration and presence. Sometimes you may need to guide your child out into the yard so that she can hit the ground with a bat, allowing her to vent her frustration and anger. At other times, she will need your help to find her tears.

Only after recognition and regulation is it possible to help our child with finding an outer-world solution (if there is one). If we jump too quickly to problem solving, we lose the opportunity the emotion has presented. Give it time. Give it space. There is much richness in these emotionally turbulent times. As Mark Epstein writes, "It is my experience that emotions, no matter how powerful, are not overwhelming if given room to breathe. Contained within the vastness of awareness, our emotions have the power to connect us with each other rather than driving us apart" (Epstein 1998, 111). By practicing self-regulation and bringing our own emotional intelligence to these situations, we will help these same qualities bloom in our children.

Mentorship as Intention and Attitude

Our intention with mentorship is to help guide our families toward greater harmony and flow, and to support our children in becoming able to steer their own ships. We create structures that we feel will support flow and predictability but not lead to suffocation. One of our main intentions is to remember that one day we will have to hand the reins over to our child. Periodically ask yourself, "Am I creating a bridge to my child's own authentic motivations and values? Or am I guiding in a way that cuts her off from her own wisdom?"

Perhaps the most important intention in being a mentor is not necessarily to have all the answers, but rather to *be* your child's answer (Neufeld and Maté 2004). When you take the disposition of a loving alpha who is committed to protecting, caring for, and guiding your child, her emotional brain—the limbic system—will relax. The feeling she has will be, "Mom has got me. I am safe and looked after." So the attitude of being an alpha is actually the most important thing when it comes to parenting. Whether you say "yes" or "no" in any given situation is often irrelevant. What matters most is that you are in the lead when it comes to the relationship, that you get where your child is coming from, and that you let her know that you are on her team. Children can handle all manner of upsets and instances of not getting their way when a loving hierarchy is established. And children trust us most when we are a grounded embodiment of presence. We can become more trustable by doing the following mindfulness awareness practice a few times a day.

Mindfulness Awareness Practice 12:
Grounding Down

Start by taking a deep breath down into your belly, allowing it to expand and fill with air. On the exhale, let the breath flow down from your belly through your pelvis and down your legs, emptying through your feet deep into the ground. Then imagine inhaling that air up from the ground, through the bottoms of your feet, up your legs, and through the pelvis, and again imagine collecting the air in the belly. Exhale down again. Do this a few times on your own.

This should help bring awareness and a sense of gravitas to the lower half of your body. It tends to calm the mind and provide a sense of solidity, of here-ness, of presence. You can also visualize yourself as a tree, exhaling down into the earth, with long, deep roots that stabilize and anchor you. Inhale up the roots, imagining your feet and legs and belly are the trunk of the tree: solid and unshakable.

We can ground down almost anywhere—while standing in line at the grocery store, watching our child play at the park, or stirring pasta at the stove. With practice, we begin to feel and walk with a more grounded sense of confidence. How we carry ourselves makes a huge difference in how safe our children feel and how much they trust our guidance.

Summary

Children need trustable adults in their lives in order to guide them toward healthy habits, strong values, and the development of emotional intelligence. They need our help in developing the capacities and qualities that lie dormant and unseen within them. When we become mindful parents, we will know when to intervene in a helpful way and when to sit back and let things take their course. With one eye on harmony in the home, and the other on the development of self-discipline, we parents grow by feeling our way along and focusing on becoming the change we want to see.

9.

HEALTHY BOUNDARIES

Encouraging Impulse Control and Adaptability

God, grant me the serenity to accept the things I cannot change; courage to change the things I can; and wisdom to know the difference.

—Reinhold Niebuhr, "The Serenity Prayer"

Four-year-old Lola loved that chocolate chip cookie, and she wanted another. Her mother said, "No, sweetheart. Not tonight." On another night, her mom might have given her a second cookie, but it was bedtime and Lola had been really out of sorts today. Lola implored, "Pleeaase, I want another cookie!" Mom said firmly, "No. No more tonight. It is time for bed." Lola got angry and started to throw a tantrum. Intuitively putting a touch of sadness in her voice, Mom said, "I know, darling. You really wanted it. I am sorry, baby." Lola started to cry. Her mom moved in and scooped her up into her lap, supporting the full weight of her body. She breathed deeply as she held Lola, saying very little except an occasional, "I know…" or "Oh, sweetheart.…" She could feel her heart breaking right along with Lola's.

After about twenty or thirty seconds, the sobs began to wind themselves down and Lola released that final long exhale that comes at the end of a good cry. And then, stillness. After a moment of silence, Lola leaned back and looked deeply into her mother's eyes, her face softer and more relaxed than it had been all day. They gazed at each other for what felt like a timeless eternity.

Setting limits can be one of the hardest parts of parenting. We have all had experiences of unnecessarily being restrained, controlled, and manipulated, and many of us have vowed to never do that to our children. But boundaries don't merely restrict us. Paradoxically, boundaries help us mature and lead us to greater freedom.

Parenting is primarily about creating a container of safety for our children, which in part requires clear and loving boundaries. When our child knows what to expect, she relaxes. When she learns to rein in her impulses for those she loves, she feels increasingly proud of the person she is becoming. When she faces the unavoidable limits that we all face, and learns how to stay present with vulnerable emotions, she emerges as a more emotionally resilient, courageous, and heartfelt person. An important part of parenting is helping children learn how to handle limits gracefully and experience them as opportunities for growth.

What Are Healthy Boundaries?

Boundaries stop flow in a particular direction only to increase flow in another. Picture the banks of a river. Without the banks, the water would spill over chaotically and flood the plains. The banks help channel the flow of water down to the sea.

Some boundaries are placed on us by life—we didn't win the soccer championship, we didn't get invited to the sleepover we wanted to go to, or we can't bring our dog back to life. Other times the limits come directly from the adults in charge. In parenting, part of our responsibility is to help guide the flow of our children's instinctual energy into safe and appropriate expressions. Sometimes we stop a particular behavior to prevent physical harm to our children or to others. Other times we step in to protect their minds from being filled with too much violence and fear. And there are also times when we need to stop children from a futile course of action, simply to help them become capable of accepting the things they cannot change.

How Boundaries Nourish

Diana Baumrind's research found that children who grow up in homes without adequate boundaries had less impulse control and poorer self-regulation, were more self-centered and less socially competent, and had lower achievement motivation and cognitive performance (Grolnick 2009). The easiest way to think about this is that when children do not have a parent who is clearly in the lead, they feel uncontained, unheld, and more out of control. In short, they feel less safe. This increases their limbic reactivity and interferes with self-regulation, cognition, learning, and relating to others effectively.

To be clear, we are not talking about being overly controlling or harsh with our children. We are talking about setting limits for *their* sake. Sometimes they will benefit directly, like when we intervene for their safety and health. At other times they will benefit over the long term by being asked to practice impulse control and become adaptive to the realities of life, and thereby grow up capable and resilient. And in other moments they will benefit indirectly from boundaries that are necessary to meet the more pressing needs of another family member. As a family, we rise and fall together with each other's moods and happiness. Everyone deserves respect and consideration. As the old saying goes, "If momma ain't happy, ain't no one happy." (This, of course, applies to us daddies too.) Let's look at three ways healthy boundaries nourish our children: enhancing their safety and health, building their impulse control and response flexibility, and fostering their ability to adapt in the face of adversity.

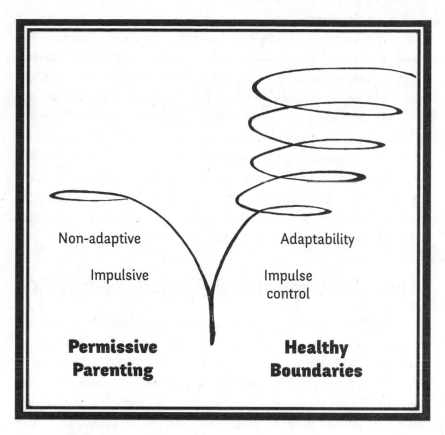

Figure 8: The Fruits of Healthy Boundaries

Safety and Health

Our first charge as parents is to keep our children safe and healthy. When your infant grabs a nickel off the counter and puts it in her mouth, you may lovingly say, "Oh no, baby girl...not in your mouth," and remove the coin from her grasp. When your toddler bolts from your side and is inches away from getting hit by cross traffic, grabbing his arm and pulling him to safety is a must. This clear and decisive limit—and the stern verbal lesson that might appropriately follow—is an intelligent response when faced with this normal but dangerous expression of a child's immaturity. Love is protective.

We are also responsible for our children's health. Sometimes parents suggest that children, when allowed to follow their own instincts, will find their way to what their body needs; that we do not need to interfere with their choices. Sometimes this is true; often it is not. Most children will choose ice cream and cookies over carrots if given the chance, and only rarely do I hear about children putting themselves to bed at a decent hour in order to get enough rest for the following day. Structures such as healthy meals, regular bedtime routines, and reasonable limitations on TV and exposure to violent imagery are gifts to our children, not punishments. As Brian Swimme writes, "Every child needs to learn this simple truth: she is the energy of the sun. And we adults should organize things so her face shines with the same radiant joy" (1996, 42).

Impulse Control and Response Flexibility

Through our loving support, children can be invited to practice exercising in the arena of self-discipline. Self-discipline at a minimum requires controlling impulses that are harmful and choosing responses that are in alignment with our values and aspirations. Self-control has been linked with a variety of positive outcomes such as better health, higher SAT scores, higher income levels, better social skills, and greater levels of happiness (Lieberman 2013). Without self-discipline, our children will remain impulsive creatures not capable of considering the effects of their behavior on others or on their own future.

If your toddler is hitting you, and that behavior is straining the relationship, it becomes your responsibility to guide him toward expressing his frustration in a less harmful way. "We can hit pillows when we are frustrated, but not people" is an example of guiding our child in a way that helps him stay in touch with his inner world of feelings while simultaneously inviting him to exercise his developing prefrontal cortex (PFC) "muscle." Without the boundary of "no hitting people," and the guidance of "we *can* hit pillows," the PFC does not get exercised and remains weak. Over time, this translates into more strained relationships and less steadfastness toward mastery in many arenas of life. Your child will become less *competent* without boundaries, and by extension, less *confident.* Loving guidance invites children to develop into their fullest potential.

Limits are most effectively set when they are firm, clear, and come from a grounded sense of authority. This does not require you to be unkind, but it does require that you are solid and centered. Many times we try to win the argument by "climbing on top": getting big and scary and trying to energetically push the child down into submission. But children see through this. Part of them might become afraid because you are losing your cool, but another part of them is feeling, "This is working! Mom is losing her center. I have a chance here."

When you feel your energy boiling up into your head, recall the "grounding down" practice we introduced in the last chapter. Slow down. Inhale warm air into your belly, and exhale it down through your legs, feet, and into the earth. Establish a connection with the earth and a sense of solidity. Speak less. And when you do speak, deliver the message from your belly: clearly, slowly, and firmly. You are the adult here. Trust that you know what is best. Keep your heart and ears open, but trust yourself and your ability to make wise and loving decisions. Don't let your child's emotional storm uproot you.

Know Where Your Power Lies

Sometimes we get into the worst power struggles because we do not pick the right spots to assert our authority. Boundaries are more effectively set in some circumstances than in others. If you try to assert your authority in places you do not have the power, you will only reveal your impotence or become belligerent out of frustration and feelings of powerlessness.

Boundaries are most effectively set where your child needs *your help*, not the other way around. You can't really make him eat or rake the leaves without physically forcing him to move his body. So don't put excessive pressure and aggression into trying to make these behaviors happen. Instead, tell him what you would like to see happen and give space for him to step into the decision. If he does not eat his meal, but then asks for ice cream, now you have some power. "No, sweetheart. We can't put a bunch of sugar into our bodies without first eating healthy food. I am sorry." Or "No. I am not taking you to soccer practice tonight. You have reneged on your promise to get those leaves raked for a whole week now. Sorry, but respect is a two-way street."

So pick your spots better and you will experience less frustration, anger, and guilt.

Adaptiveness in the Face of Adversity

The adaptive process is "the process by which we are changed by that which we cannot change" (Neufeld and Maté 2004). We all face limits in life: our own limits of physical form and functioning, limits placed on us by people and society, and things we cannot control, like pain and loss. It becomes essential that we learn to find our feelings of disappointment and our tears of sadness around the things in life that cannot be changed. Becoming adaptive to reality is an essential life skill. It is not what happens to us, but how we navigate the troubled waters of life that matters most. Without adaptation, we become hardened, less resilient, and less fulfilled.

The adaptive process deserves an entire book of its own, but we will try to briefly outline the key steps here. Let's refer back to the vignette at the beginning of this chapter as an example. Lola's mother felt that it was not in her best interest to have another cookie before bed. She presented a clear boundary by saying "No." As Lola protested, her mother made clear the futility of her protest by staying firm and not getting into a debate with her. She then put a touch of sadness in her voice, trying to precipitate feelings of sadness and disappointment in Lola. Once Lola started to cry, she moved in to hold and comfort her in her experience of vulnerability. She held Lola closely but spaciously, giving her all the time she needed for the tears to naturally wind themselves down. She knew the process was complete when Lola released that long exhale and became still. And then her daughter emerged softer, cleaned out, and refreshed through her good cry.

Too often we avoid tears, or try to short-circuit them, believing they are traumatic. But they are not traumatic. In fact, when experienced in safe and loving arms, they are protective. It is important that we begin to see how essential and transformative tears really are. As Washington Irving once said, "There is a sacredness in tears. They are the mark not of weakness, but of power. They speak more eloquently than ten thousand tongues. They are messengers of overwhelming grief...and of unspeakable love" (quoted in Bate, 1888, 832).

The gifts of becoming adaptive are many. Children develop better self-regulation and better impulse control, and are less aggressive. Adaptive children learn from their mistakes and are more self-correcting. They are better able to transcend their handicaps and shortcomings, and accept guidance from mentors. They are less reactive and less defensive; their hearts are softer. Neuroscientists are now confirming what developmental psychologists have been observing for many years: when the emotional system is open, vital, and fluid, maturation proceeds most easefully. A soft heart is the basis for emotional intelligence, resilience, and the development of maturity (Neufeld and Maté 2004).

Resilience and Thriving

There are "survive" forms of resilience and there are "thrive" forms of resilience. The thrive form of resilience comes in two gears: the upshift and the downshift.

The upshift form of resilience is when we experience some adversity and stress, stay focused and regulated, draw on our resources, overcome the obstacle, and reach our goal. This is the resilience we need to give a speech when we are scared, to perform well on a stressful entrance exam, or to work things out with an angry friend.

The downshift form of resilience is when we finally accept the truth: in this moment, we cannot get what we want. We can't win. Instead, we sink into our vulnerable feelings: disappointment, sadness, loss, powerlessness, and so on. Fully feeling our vulnerability, we become transformed from the inside out. We then can reapproach the situation with a newfound perspective, wisdom, and heart. This is the adaptive process and is a key contributor to resilience.

A soft heart is also essential for true fulfillment in life. We can't fully know joy without experiencing our sadness. We cannot come to really appreciate who and what we have unless we have been submerged in loss. We can't truly exude compassion until we have been rocked by feelings like pain and rejection. Without experiencing the empty and vulnerable territory of the human heart we will never quite feel satisfied, nor deeply fulfilled. As Léon Bloy said, "There are places in the heart that do not yet exist. Suffering has to enter in for them to come to be" (Calhoun, 2011, 166).

Each time we accept the things we cannot change, we increase our capacity for emotional resilience. Each confrontation with our inherent vulnerability brings us one step closer to what Chögyam Rinpoche called "unconditional confidence" (Chödrön 2009). This is not the confidence that we will always get our way and always be able to change the environment or ourselves into what we think is best. Rather, it is the confidence that we will be able to handle—and be grown up by—whatever circumstances we find ourselves in. We begin to trust life itself more than our judgments. We begin to trust our ability to be in direct contact with our experience, no matter how scary. It is our ability to be with our "shaky tenderness" that ultimately delivers us into our unconditional confidence (Chödrön 1994, 72). Our children are completely capable of adapting. Let's not sell them short.

Note that adaptation is not the same thing as accommodation. *Accommodation* is when we feel pressure from our loved ones to be someone other than who we are. When parents disapprove and withhold their love when their baby cries or their toddler becomes angry, the children will begin to repress parts of themselves to get the food and the love. *Adaptation* does not require the child to desire, feel, or be anything other than what she is. It simply puts a boundary on what happens in the physical world. Wanting a third cookie before bed is fine, but it doesn't mean you can have one. When children come up against limits and have a good cry, they don't become more closed down, as is the case in accommodation; they become more emotionally open and resilient.

Healthy Boundaries in Everyday Life

There are two basic types of limit setting: ordinary limit setting and limits set for the purpose of adaptation. Ordinary limits are by far the most common, but in the toddler and preschool years, adaptative limit setting can and should occur often (Neufeld and Maté 2004). Children's emotional systems are open and fluid early in their lives, and the adaptive process helps them stay that way.

Ordinary Limit Setting

Ordinary limit setting involves strategies to work with our children within a particular boundary and keep things relatively copacetic. We are trying to maintain flow and harmony, as well as help our children become more self-disciplined along the way. Through using distraction, choice, and providing rationales for our limits we evoke less counterwill, teach our children about cooperation, and help them strengthen their prefrontal cortex.

Especially with younger children, we may set a limit and then distract them. When a one-year-old reaches for an electrical plug, we may say, "No-no, baby girl...look at this," as we hand her a red rubber ball.

We may set a limit subtly by giving choice: "Do you want to wear the red pants or the blue pants?" This works well for the first few years, as children feel like they have some autonomy. The boundary—you are wearing pants—is invisible to the young child, in the background.

Another way to set limits is to state the limit and give clear explanations and our rationale: "You can't play with J. J. over in his fort because I can't see or hear you. It is too far." This gives your child the information he needs to understand "why" and begin coming up with win-win solutions increasingly on his own: "Well, can we play in our backyard on the trampoline?" Giving explanations also helps him see your perspective and this helps him recognize that you are not trying to control him unnecessarily. He hears your concerns and begins to understand that you are trying to meet as many requests as possible within reason.

Limit Setting for Adaptation

Limits set to support adaptation are different. Instead of helping our child upshift and find a suitable solution, we are trying to bring her down into her vulnerability so that she becomes transformed and made more resilient in the process. Vulnerable feelings like disappointment, sadness, loss, and powerlessness are feelings our survival-oriented egos would rather avoid. But it is through the doorway of adaptation that we become more courageous, authentic, loving, and free. The adaptive process is essential if we are to thrive.

It is important to point out that adaptation is primarily an emotional process, not a rational one. We want to keep our words short and to the point, and avoid getting dragged into a debate. Firmness and clarity are the keys to halting your child's attempts at manipulation. Compassion is the key to drawing the energy down into the heart and precipitating the tears.

Here we want to distinguish between two types of compassion. In the adaptive process, we are not going for *emotional compassion,* where we try to make the child feel better by saying "It will be all right," giving him what he wants, or trying to distract him from his vulnerable feelings with some cool, shiny object. Too much emotional compassion communicates to a child, "You cannot handle reality and the pain that sometimes comes with it."

When we are supporting the adaptive process, we try to help him fully feel his vulnerable feelings and stay with the truth of his experience. Hameed Ali puts it this way: "The point of compassion is not to eliminate suffering, but to lead a person to truth so that she will be able to live a life of truth…Compassion is a kind of healing agent that helps us tolerate the hurt of seeing the truth…It is only when compassion is present that people allow themselves to see the truth" (Almaas 1987, 85). Our role is to feel our child's vulnerability from the heart, communicate compassion, and become a safe haven where he can cry. Let's look at an example to see how this might look in real life.

A nine-year-old girl named Lela really wants to go to a sleepover party that she was not invited to. She is visibly agitated and starts pressuring her parents to take her over to the girl's house. "I want to go over there; they must have forgotten to invite me. Pleeaase just drive me over there."

"No, I am so sorry, darling. She didn't invite you," her mother replies.

"But…"

"No, sweetie. It's not going to happen."

Lela starts to yell. "I hate you! You never help me with anything. You're not on my side. I wish I didn't belong to this family!"

Her mother doesn't react. Instead she says, "I am so sorry, my love. I am really sorry. I know it hurts…" as she is feeling the pain in her own heart.

149

And then Lela throws herself on her bed and begins to cry. Her mother moves in to hold her. She pulls Lela's head onto her lap and cradles her while she goes through wave after wave of sobbing. Mom says little and does little to interfere; she just holds her. She is as heartbroken as Lela is. "I know, baby...I know..." she says as she feels a gaping hole in her chest.

With time, the sobs begin to wind themselves down. And then the long exhale, and then the still point. The entire room feels very alive and spacious. The two are completely present, their bodies relaxed and pressed against each other. This kind of closeness has become more and more rare, and they are both soaking in the moment.

Mom strokes Lela's hair as they talk a little bit about the situation. There is still hurt in their hearts, but the pain is slowly being subsumed by a deep love and quiet strength. Neither of them wants to move. The fullness of the moment nourishes them both.

This process is challenging, but it is so important. Its steps are easy to outline, but in real life they must flow from you intuitively in the moment. You find yourself in a situation where a boundary is the most healthy thing, where it is in the child's best interest. You set the boundary clearly and firmly, hold her in the futility, and then put a touch of sadness in your voice and hope she is ready and willing to sink into her tears. If she is not, there is nothing you can do. This cannot be forced, only invited. Once she does begin to feel her vulnerable feelings, you become a grounded, spacious, and loving holding place for her to fully let go into.

Be supportive, but try not to interfere too much out of your own discomfort. Hold, touch, and talk in a way that works for the particular child, in the particular moment. Stay present as long as it takes to reach the still point. And when the still point comes, enjoy it. It is a rich, pregnant time.

And lastly, enjoy whatever space your child emerges into. Sometimes she will be very peaceful, other times vibrant. Many times you will feel a palpable difference in the degree of emotional intimacy between you. Often your child will share things with you that she had previously not been talking about: some intimate details of her life, some vulnerable feelings she has been hiding. Anxious children are often much calmer for a while after a good cycle of adaptation. Children who are somewhat aggressive usually lose their edge for a period of time. A good cry has a way of draining tension and resetting limbic reactivity.

This process is the same whether your toddler is upset about not getting a cookie, your grade-schooler does not make the baseball team, or your preteen is crushed over grandma's passing. Each time we pass into the vulnerable territory of the heart and survive it, our nervous system registers that "I can handle not getting my way. It feels like I am going to die, but by now I have survived these confrontations hundreds of times. I am stronger and more resilient than I ever imagined." Adaptation becomes the basis for a true and lasting courage. By helping our children exercise the brain circuitry of adaptation, we equip them to survive the unavoidable crises of life and buffer them from becoming traumatized by those crises. We can only physically protect our children for so long. Helping them cultivate emotional resilience is one of the greatest gifts we can give them for their journey.

There is nothing more supportive than having safe, loving arms to sink into when we are feeling vulnerable. Part of being a loving alpha is providing that container for our children. In the mindfulness awareness practice that follows, we bring together three of the practices you have already learned: grounding down (chapter eight), getting spacious (chapter seven), and feeling from the heart (chapter five).

Mindfulness Awareness Practice 13:
A Safe Place to Cry

The next time you have to set a boundary with your child, set it clearly and succinctly. Then, put a touch of sadness into your voice and, when your child begins to sink into her tears, move in to hold her. For a younger child, scoop her up into your lap and support her weight fully. The more you are holding and supporting her, the more she can let go into the emotion. As she is crying on your shoulder, you can rotate your breath through each of the three practices.

Inhale into your belly, exhale down through the lower half of your body, and become rooted to the ground—stable in the face of this emotional storm. Inhale from the ground into your belly and chest, and exhale out in all directions, dissolving your awareness out into the spaciousness of the room that can give this process all the space and time it needs to unfold in its own intelligent way. And then breathe your child directly into your heart. Feel her vulnerability, her pain, fully. And on the exhale, feel the love and compassion flowing from your heart effortlessly, the out-breath simply emptying out the natural response of the heart.

Feel her body close to yours, its size and shape, a fleeting expression that will be gone in the blink of an eye. Be solid and spacious for her, but relish the experience as well. These are among the most intimate and heart-opening experiences of our lives. Let the power of heartbreak and compassion saturate every cell in your body.

Consequences

There will be times when we have tried everything to get our children on board with our decisions, but they still choose not to comply. Sometimes we agree to disagree and let it go. Other times we feel it is important enough to apply a little more pressure. Ultimately, we cannot abdicate our responsibilities. As Martin Luther King, Jr., once said, "power without love is reckless and abusive," and "love without power is sentimental and anemic" (1967).

Children learn best from the consequences of their actions. If at all possible, we try and let them learn from the *natural consequences* that life provides. This way their autonomy is preserved and we don't have to be the bad guys. We may let them forget their lunch instead of nagging them every day, and have the hunger do the reminding. We may let them turn in a sloppy paper and allow the teacher's response to be what motivates them to do a better job the next go-around. In this way, we can stay on "their team," helping to support them and find solutions, if and when they want us to.

But sometimes we can't allow natural consequences to take place. If the consequence is dangerous to the child (allowing her to run into traffic and risk getting hit by a car) or to another person (letting him throw rocks at the park and risking another child getting hit on the head), we may have to intervene and be clear about a boundary and the consequence that will follow. This is called creating a *logical consequence*.

We may say, "Selim, if you throw a rock again, we are going to have to leave the park. There are too many children here and someone might get hurt." You get his buy-in: "You know what I am saying?" He replies, "Yeah." "Thanks, buddy," you say, and return to the park bench with your friend and keep your fingers crossed.

The consequence is not meant to punish or unnecessarily hurt Selim. It is simply part of safe park protocol. The consequence is reasonable, related to the action, and delivered in a way that is respectful. This is what distinguishes consequences from punishments (Nelsen 1981). Punishments are intended to hurt the person, to make them suffer to excess. Punishments are more about retribution and vengeance than finding balance and justice. They don't work as well in the long run because the hurt evokes resistance and the desire to get revenge, and creates more sneakiness and lying. It also ultimately hurts the relationship, which is your best chance to draw your child toward being self-disciplined for the right reasons.

As we have been saying, the ideal is to create a boundary and give your child choice within that boundary. Let her come up with possible solutions that meet both of your desires. Once a win-win has been created, make an agreement about the consequence if the agreement is broken. Here again, let your child take a shot at creating the consequence. You have ultimate say about what you think will actually work, but when your child creates the consequence he is much more likely to follow through. He has a lot more buy-in, having been a key part of the process. The tow of you agree together that if he throws any more rocks, you'll both have to leave the park. "Got it?" you ask.

"Got it," he replies. This is a better option than exploding in anger and punishing him. Instead, you become proactive and made a clear agreement, and now you can relax and stop nagging.

Healthy Boundaries as Intention and Attitude

Our primary intention with boundary setting is to help our children develop their upshift and their downshift capacities. And perhaps most importantly, we want them to develop "the wisdom to know the difference," to borrow from the serenity prayer. We want them to be able to recognize when it is time to dig deep, be courageous, and stick to something that is difficult. And we want them to also recognize when to downshift into acceptance of the outer situation—to give up the fight and sink into the vulnerable feelings that are evoked. This wisdom is one of the fruits of mindfulness and of maturity.

The *attitude* needed here is to try and embody this wisdom every day. The more mindful, grounded, and heart-centered we are, the more we will recognize the truth of what is needed in the moment. Many times we will have to hold a boundary with ourselves: "I know you want to wring his little neck, but stay cool." We often need to keep ourselves regulated and behaving respectfully, hour after hour, day after day, in order to lovingly serve our children as they are growing up. Other times we will have to stop trying to make it all work for our children. We will need to find our grief over having neglected ourselves and/or our relationship for so long, and restore some balance to our lives.

We love our children so much that we want things to be perfect for them. But many things in parenting don't work out the way we want them to. That is an unavoidable aspect of the job, and of life itself. If we are not able to find *our* tears, how can we expect our children to find *theirs*? We must continue to become adaptive ourselves, lest we harden ourselves in this time when our families need tenderness the most.

Summary

Part of our job as parents is to help steer our children toward what works and away from what does not. Healthy boundaries keep our children safe and vibrant, promote the development of impulse control and response flexibility, and help them become adaptive in the face of adversity. Drawing again on the serenity prayer, our children need to develop "the serenity to accept the things [they] cannot change; courage to change the things [they] can; and wisdom to know the difference." Through our mindful, loving presence, we can put our children on a clear path toward true courage, wisdom, and the invincible vulnerability of the human heart.

10.

MIS-TAKES

The Gifts of Compassion, Humility, and Forgiveness

Your exact errors make a music
that nobody hears.

—William Stafford, "You and Art"

Simon's three-year-old son is messing with the dog's bowl, and spills water all over the floor. He has been alone with both of his boys all week and this puts him over the edge. He yells at his son: "What the hell is the matter with you? Get out of here!" Cole scrambles upstairs and yells back at his father, "NO!" swinging his little arm.

"Don't you 'no' me!" Simon says as Cole disappears around the corner. Simmering, he begins to clean up yet another mess. Simon is really frustrated. He is frustrated with the never-ending messes and cleanup duty. And he is also frustrated with himself: "Why can't I handle this better? He is just three. It was probably an accident. Cut him some slack," he thinks to himself. And then an insight appears. Some compassionate voice deep within him whispers, "This is hard. It has been a long day. It has been a long week. It's okay…" Simon begins to soothingly rub his hand over his heart: "It's okay. You are doing your best," he says to himself. "Hang in there. This is hard."

He visualizes one of his teachers sitting in the room, looking at him with a soft, loving, steady gaze. He feels the compassion and the kindness in his teacher's gaze. He feels seen by his mentor, and he feels his vote of confidence in his abilities. Simon feels his eyes water and his body soften. He takes a deep breath, lets out a long exhale, and starts upstairs.

He comes alongside his son while he is playing quietly at his train table. "Hey buddy, I'm sorry I yelled at you. Daddy was really frustrated when the water spilled. I am really tired and worn out and when I saw the water all over the floor I got all crazy. Daddy was like a big bear, huh? 'Rrroooaaar!'" he says, doing his best bear imitation. Cole smiles. Simon continues, "And then you yelled back at daddy, huh? You yelled, 'NO!' And daddy said, 'Don't you "no" me!'" He says all of this in an animated, playful re-creation. Both laugh together, and then Cole leans in to his daddy. Simon just holds his boy—no words—just breathing together; the quiet intimacy more healing than words.

The myth of "perfect parenting" needs to be shattered. There is not, and never has been, a parent who never stepped out of line—not even close. There is also no one style of communication or one approach to parenting that leads in a direct line to maturity. Development is a long and winding road—always a work in progress, always full of potholes and construction zones—and it doesn't end just because we have become a parent. If we insist on total order and obedience, or if we think we are supposed to always "do it right," we will set ourselves—and our children—up for years of frustration and resentment.

Parenting is more like a dance than a straight sprint from here to there. And when we dance, we sometimes step on toes. We must trust that the music animating us and our children has its own rhythm and timing: that each part of the song has its own purpose that contributes to the whole. Then, maybe, we can relax our grip a little bit and see what wants to be born through us in each moment. To our judges, mis-takes are something to be avoided. But the seed inside of every living soul needs more than sunlight, air, and water in order to thrive. It needs the manure of life to grow up vital, robust, and whole.

What Are Mis-takes?

Usually we call something a *mistake* when it is out of alignment with what we think is right—what we think *should* happen. Notice that there is some element of judgment inherent in calling something a "mistake." According to some system of evaluation, it indicates we think something is bad or wrong. But should we take our judges at their word? Should we assume things are actually not going the way they are supposed to just because our judge hands down the assessment that "this is wrong"?

Evaluation is a normal and healthy part of mental functioning. We need assessments of what works and what does not. We need guidelines for appropriate interactions in various situations. But when we operate from the mindset of the judge, healthy evaluation—which naturally has elements of openness and responsiveness—can stiffen into dogmatic rigidity. Judging the world and ourselves, we lose the true complexity of the moment. We lose our capacity to see the situation from multiple perspectives. And worst of all, we lose our humanity.

The Chinese symbol for "crisis" is comprised of two characters: one signifying "danger" and the other "opportunity." To our judge, this territory is definitely to be avoided. But a deeper part of every human being is always on the lookout for an authentic tussle with what is real, even if it feels uncomfortable. "Mis-takes" is our word for things that happen in the territory that lies outside of our visualized "ideal," but holds enormous opportunity for learning, compassion, and intimacy.

How Mis-takes Nourish

There are several reasons why mis-takes—especially when followed up with kindness and humility—are actually very nourishing to your child's developing psyche. When children experience the unavoidable misattunements and pains of relational life in the care of parents who are able to make heartfelt repairs, these wounds can be transformed into compassion, for oneself and for others who are also struggling. Mis-takes also help children learn how to move beyond rigid idealism into a humility grounded in the truth of how things actually are. And lastly, mis-takes provide opportunies for our children to experience and practice forgiveness: the act of countering shame and pain through heartfelt vulnerabilty and connection.

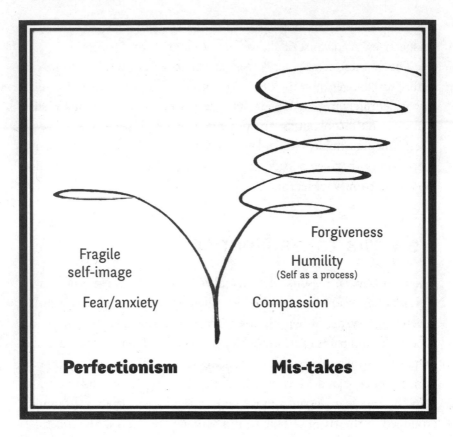

Perfectionism

Fragile
self-image

Fear/anxiety

Forgiveness

Humility
(Self as a process)

Compassion

Mis-takes

Figure 9: The Fruits of Mis-takes

Compassion

The science of attachment has brought heightened awareness of how chronic misattunements can negatively impact a child's developing brain. A misattunement is when people do not properly read and reflect to us that they understand us. We do not feel seen or felt. Because of our need for connection, our nervous system registers this as some degree of threat: the threat of separation and abandonment. When prolonged, this can be especially dysregulating for infants. Babies do not yet have enough experience to reassure them that they will not be abandoned, nor the capacities of self-regulation to help stabilize them in their time of need. The first year is a time when infants especially benefit from mindful attunement.

And yet this knowledge can be taken to an extreme that is unhelpful. Many parenting philosophies have drawn distorted conclusions from the research and left many parents overly anxious about causing damage to their children by not being 100 percent attuned, 24/7. The truth is that misattunements happen and happen often, and at normal levels they actually fuel our growth. In parent-child relationships with *secure attachment*—the ones most likely to shape children into emotionally intelligent beings—misattunements occur around every nineteen seconds on average (Wallin 2007). Clearly, at this level, misattunements are not a problem for normal human development.

These misattunements are part of our training for the real world, where people will not always be attuned and empathic. Good but imperfect attunement is exactly what children need (Wallin 2007); this is what developmental pediatrician D. W. Winnicott called "good enough mothering" (1964, 240). Recall that there is actually an optimal level of frustration that promotes resilience.

When a parent is mostly attuned to a child, the child's predominant *mental model* (a set of expectations we carry in our minds) is, "Daddy sees, understands, and responds to me." This sets up an implicit expectation in the child's mind that she is likely to get attunement from those she is close to out in the world. In the moments when daddy isn't attuned to her, but recovers and reconnects after the disruption is noticed, she begins to develop a second important model in her mind: "Ruptures are not life-threatening and are usually followed up by reconnection." This second mental model helps her feel safe and resilient out in the world, where ruptures will occur more frequently. When we recover from misattunements—especially in emotionally turbulent times—and reconnect with our child, she develops the faith that it is possible to have disconnects and find our way back to love.

Out of these experiences, compassion is born. Children come to know the pain of separation as well as their desire to be healed in reconnection. They begin to intuitively sense the imperfections of life as opportunities to return to the heart. The momentary disruptions are like sand in the oyster that instigates the formation of the pearl—in this case, the pearl is compassion.

Humility, not Perfectionism

Growing up in a home with a parent who is trying to be perfect, and trying to make everyone else fit her ideal of perfection, is stressful. The home is full of tension. Everyone is on edge, feeling like they are always being watched and judged. This keeps a child's nervous system chronically in the survive mode, because the love feels conditional. There is no rest, only chronic vigilance and control followed by bursts of reactivity. No one thrives when they've been made into a project.

When you allow room in your home and life for spills and outbursts, and when you acknowledge your own missteps without making a big deal of it, children get the message that messiness is part of life. Your being more accepting of life's hiccups helps children relax into the thrive mode, where they are better able to see what went awry, right their own ship, and learn from their mis-takes.

Accepting imperfection as part of life helps remind us that we are dynamic—continually learning and growing—as opposed to static, fixed entities. Responding to messiness and missteps gracefully helps our children see themselves as a process and promotes humility. Through humility, we return to the ground of our being whose fundamental nature is change. Research by Stanford University professor of psychology Carol Dweck (discussed in Pink 2009) shows that it is advantageous for our children to develop a "growth mindset" as opposed to a "fixed mindset" when it comes to learning and becoming more competent. A growth mindset is one where "failures" are seen as an unavoidable and necessary part of learning, whereas a fixed mindset sees them as damaging to one's self-image. Helping our children see themselves clearly—their strengths and their weaknesses—allows them to move toward the thrive-side growth mindset (Pink 2009; see appendix D for more).

A Range of Emotion

Children need experience with a wide range of emotions in order to develop emotional intelligence. They need to know that each emotion has a place and a purpose, and that they can trust the flow of energy within them. Appropriate expression also takes a long time to develop. But the key—especially in the early years—is to make room for the full repertoire of emotions. This is why we believe being authentic is more valuable than tightly controlling and suppressing our emotions around our children.

Emotions have a lot to teach us about ourselves, and about the interior landscapes of others. It is helpful for children to see their parents be authentic yet respectful in communicating their emotions. In the process, things will get messy at times. But don't they get messy anyway? Do people who suppress their emotions avoid blowups? Do they never go off the deep end? No. In fact suppression and repression often make the blowups worse. It is important that we as parents bring a mindful attention to our experience and allow emotions to reveal themselves and teach us what is really going on below the surface. In this way, we stand the best chance of consciously working with our inner demons rather than unconsciously discharging them all over our children and our partners.

It is important to note, however, that we must bring great care and sensitivity to our emotional expression. We don't want to lay a guilt trip on our children and make them feel responsible for our emotions; they are not. No one is responsible for our emotions; they are an inherent part of the body-brain package we were born with. Like development itself, emotions have their own logic, rhythm, and timing. The more clearly we can see the actual causes and conditions that give rise to circumstances, the less emotionally reactive we will be. Here again, mindfulness practice is of enormous benefit. When we are able to see our emotions clearly and attend to them, we are better able to express ourselves with skill and care. When our children see us consciously working with difficult emotions like hurt, frustration, and overwhelm, they learn through our example. Sometimes we can inspire our children in the most ordinary of ways simply by living our lives with integrity—by being authentic and considerate simultaneously.

Being authentic and allowing our emotions to flow will certainly result in some messiness and mis-takes. This is okay. When children see us in an authentic struggle with our own emotions, it takes some of the pressure off them to be perfect and controlled. As John Gottman says, "A mother who finally gives herself permission to get angry is in a much better position to allow her son to have the same feeling. Once a father can acknowledge his own sadness, he's far more capable of listening to his son's or daughter's sadness" (1997, 81).

Pain, Growth, and Forgiveness

Lastly and most mysteriously, difficult experiences often spawn our most profound periods of growth. To echo the gardening metaphor we used in the first chapters of this book, manure is an ideal fertilizer. Most of us have had events in our lives that were painful, and sometimes devastating. At the time of the event, we are often caught in the difficult emotions it generates. But sometimes—maybe a year later, or maybe a decade—what we endured all of a sudden makes sense to us. We see how we were changed in some fundamental and significant way by our confrontation with reality. We see how we would never have had a particular insight or perspective had we not experienced the difficulty. We see how perfect it was after all.

The same is true for the wounds we inevitably acquire in childhood. The ways that our parents cannot see us, the ways they want us to be different than we are, the ways we were all left unfulfilled in our childhoods—these inform us. They sensitize us and teach us about specific difficulties that human beings have to face on the road toward maturity and wholeness. It is often said that the wounds are where the gifts are. In no other place is this more true than in the parent-child relationship.

In recognizing the intelligence of the process, our hearts move toward forgiveness. We become softened as we recognize that everyone is doing their best. We choose to free ourselves from the prison of pain, hatred, and obsessive rumination. As Jack Kornfield says, "Forgiveness means giving up all hope of a better past….In the end, forgiveness simply means never putting another person out of our heart" (2002, 25, 31).

Mis-takes in Everyday Life

There are plenty of opportunities to work with our mis-takes. Sometimes the missteps are our own. Other times they are delivered by life itself, and we parents are here to help our children land more softly: to learn how to turn the manure of life into nourishing soil. In the pages that follow are some tools and principles that can help you strengthen your ability to work with mis-takes—and to help your children grow through them.

Don't Shoot the Second Arrow

Messiness and mishaps happen many times every day. The trick is to keep our judge and reactivity from piling on to the original mis-take and making things worse. Eastern philosophy teaches us that life shoots the first arrow, creating a wound, but it is our ego and our judge that shoot the second, third, and fourth arrows into the wound. Our task is to wisely and compassionately attend to the wound of the first arrow instead of spending our energy blaming, judging, or shaming ourselves for the mis-take and adding more suffering to the mix. Learning how to relax around the mis-take is crucial.

Your six-year-old accidentally spills her glass of cranberry juice on the white chair. Your body tightens and contracts. And then you see her little body contract in fear of what will happen. You pause and breathe, and say, "It was an oops." She responds, "Yes, oopsy daisy." This is the code word you two have created for when you make a mistake and do something unintentionally that upsets the other. "Come on, let's clean it up together," you say. "Messiness is just part of life." These simple, every-day encounters can show our children how to gracefully recover from mishaps, and that we are still practicing too.

"It's Not My Fault, and I Am Responsible"

One day, I (Shauna) had just returned from a conference teaching with two of my heroes in the field of mindfulness, Sylvia Boorstein and Tara Brach. One of the teachings that most touched me came from Tara, reminding us that causes and conditions lead to specific situations. She was pointing to the fact that we don't make "mistakes" on purpose—that it is our conditioning, our confusion, our fear, and our pain that lead to unskillful actions that create suffering for ourselves and others; thus, we should not beat ourselves up over them. And yet, this does not let us off the hook. Once we see clearly the pain we have caused we take responsibility, attempt to rectify any wrong, and learn from the error so that, as best we can, we do not create it again. Tara's pithy teaching was, "It's not my fault, and I am responsible."

I had recently separated from my husband, and the transition was painful for me and my four-year-old son, Jackson. Dinnertime was especially hard for us. Something felt strange, just the two of us sitting there. I decided to make a special dinner, pasta, which was Jackson's favorite. While I was cooking the pasta, Jackson was wanting to connect. Focused on making dinner, I did not give him the attention he was needing. When I finally got dinner served, he took a bite and threw his fork with food on it onto the floor, saying, "Gross. Dad's is much better."

My body contracted; I raised my voice. "Jackson, pick that up or go to your room." "No," he answered, equally loud. I stood up, took him by the hand, and walked him forcefully to his room, shutting the door loudly behind me. I returned to the kitchen to clean up the floor, and a wave of sadness and shame consumed me: "I am the worst mother. I can't even have a pleasant dinner with my son. I'm such a phony, teaching mindfulness and compassion all week and then snapping at my son at the drop of a fork!" And then Tara's teaching came back, and I realized: "It's not my fault—causes and conditions led me to this moment—and I am responsible."

I realized that while I was sitting there in the kitchen beating myself up, I could be consciously directing my attention and energy to repairing the breach with my son. I dropped the sponge, and my guilt, and returned to Jackson's room. I knelt down to the ground and hugged him. No words. Both Jackson and I knew we were wrong. And we both knew we just wanted to hold each other. I said, "I'm sorry I yelled and got so angry." Our eyes met; he still had tears in his. "I love you, Jackson. I'm sorry." We paused and let the words sink into both of us. "Do you want to come and try again?" I asked. Hand in hand, we walked back to dinner. It wasn't the night I had hoped for; however, it was a valuable experience of the power of letting go of shame, and taking responsibility.

Like it or not, strong instinctual and historical tendencies live within each of us; they are part of our inheritance. Because of this we act out, and it is not our fault. But to become wise parents we need to increasingly accept responsibility for recovering from our mis-takes with grace. One way to do this is to feel the encouragement of someone whom we know cares for us and lovingly invites us into our own tenderhearted integrity. The mindfulness awareness practice that follows helps us grow that feeling of encouragement.

Mindfulness Awareness Practice 14:
Wise Elder Visualization

Sit comfortably, eyes closed, body at ease. Feel the breath as it naturally flows in and out, setting an intention to open to all experience with a kind, curious awareness.

Call to mind a difficult interaction with your child: something that is still unresolved and has caused significant stress. Imagine you are back in the heat of the disagreement or challenge, and as vividly as possible picture yourself and your child. Imagine what words are being exchanged. Feel the emotions, tension, and stress in your body. And right in the middle of the conversation, imagine that there is a knock at the door.

You pause the conversation and go to answer the door. Standing there is a wise elder, either your older wise self, or some wise being in your life. You invite the elder in, and with great compassion, her eyes and presence communicate to you, "I see how challenging this is. I am here for you. But I have complete confidence in you."

You immediately sense the difference in your body. There is greater ease and presence. Imagine yourself, supported by the wise elder, reengaging with your child. Listen to the words you speak, the tone of your voice, your body language, and how you are feeling. Notice how your child is responding. Notice how wisdom and support bring out the best in each of you.

When you are done with the visualization, make an intention to "call in the wise elder" the next time you find yourself spiraling into reactivity with your child. Sometimes simply having a loving and encouraging presence in the room can make all the difference in the world.

Mis-takes as Intention and Attitude

There is no reason to intend to make mis-takes; they will come without trying. But we can make some intentions around how to work with ourselves and situations when mis-takes are made. The first intention we can make is to accept that something disruptive happened. Whether we have violated our own code of conduct or our child feels hurt by something we did or said, acknowledging that a boundary has been crossed and that our ship needs righting is a wise first step. Being honest and open to the truth of the situation is very important; it restores trust.

The second intention that is helpful when mis-takes are made is to bring compassion to ourselves and to any others who may have been hurt by the misstep. When we focus on bringing heart to the situation, we are less likely to judge ourselves harshly or become more belligerent or reactive with our children. Compassion and forgiveness cool the burning flames of frustration and anger and restore us to a more centered and connected place.

There are so many ways we unintentionally cause pain or are hurt by the actions of others. Feelings of guilt, shame, anger, and hatred can continue to retraumatize us long past the actual painful event. Forgiveness practice is the beginning of unlocking our hearts from the prison of self-protection. It is not meant to absolve ourselves—or others—of the responsibility to act compassionately, but rather to set the conditions from which we can be *more* compassionate in our relationships going forward. The following mindfulness awareness practice strengthens our ability to forgive and to move forward in freedom and compassion.

Mindfulness Awareness Practice 15: Forgiveness Meditation

Sit comfortably and allow your eyes to close and your breath to be natural. Allow your body to relax as you pour your awareness into it, focusing gently on the area of your heart. Begin to feel the barriers you have erected and the emotions you have held on to because you have not been able to forgive yourself or others. Allow yourself to feel the pain directly, using the guidance below. Allow the images and feelings to arise and deepen as you cultivate the heart's natural capacity to forgive. Trust the process and allow it to unfold in its own way.

The three directions of forgiveness are:

1. Asking forgiveness for harm we have caused another

2. Forgiving ourselves for self-harm

3. Forgiving another who has caused us pain

- We begin by asking Forgiveness for Hurting Another: Silently say, *There are many ways that I have hurt my child and caused her suffering, knowingly or unknowingly, out of my pain, fear, anger, and confusion.* Let yourself remember and visualize the ways you have hurt your child. See and feel the pain you have caused out of your own fear and confusion. Feel your own sorrow and regret. Picture each memory that still burdens your heart. As you are ready, silently say to your child, *I ask for your forgiveness, I ask for your forgiveness.* Allow any feelings that arise to be here. Hold them in your gentle, kind, mindful awareness. Trust the process.

- We then shift focus to Forgiveness for Hurting Ourselves: Silently say, *There are many ways that I have hurt myself. I have betrayed or abandoned myself many times through thought, word, or deed, knowingly or unknowingly.* Call to mind the ways you have hurt or harmed yourself, and allow the sorrow and pain to arise. Recognize that you can now release these burdens; it is possible to forgive yourself. As you are ready, extend forgiveness for each of these hurts. Repeat to yourself, *For the ways I have hurt myself out of fear, pain, and confusion, I now offer myself forgiveness. I forgive myself.* Continue to extend this heartfelt forgiveness as best you can, allowing any and all feelings, thoughts, and physical sensations to arise. However you are feeling is okay; you are simply inclining the heart and mind in the direction of forgiveness. Trust the process.

- Finally, we move to Forgiveness for Those Who Have Hurt Us: *There are many ways that I have been harmed, betrayed, or abandoned by others, knowingly or unknowingly, out of their confusion, fear, or pain.* Allow yourself to remember these many hurts, and feel the sorrow you have carried. Recognize that forgiving this hurt does not mean you condone it or agree with it. Forgiveness simply means that you are willing to let go of the pain and anger in your heart. As you are ready, silently repeat, *I remember the ways others have hurt or harmed me, out of fear, pain, confusion, and anger. To the extent that I am ready, I offer them forgiveness. I offer my forgiveness; I forgive you.*

For some great pains you may not feel a release; however, trust that you are planting the seeds of forgiveness, and moving in the direction of healing. Trust that you are going at the right pace and in the right way for you. Forgiveness cannot be forced. As you continue to practice the forgiveness meditation, your heart will naturally begin to let go of the past and open to the present moment.

When we bring acceptance, compassion, and forgiveness to the painful events of our lives, we find that healing begins to occur spontaneously. Intentionally bringing heart to difficult situations opens us to our inherent vulnerability. This is not the vulnerability of being susceptible and weak; this is the vulnerability that brings great strength and tenderness to our living. It is this capacity to be vulnerable that leads to a wholehearted engagement with our lives and the people in it.

These qualities are not only intentions, but are also the moment-to-moment attitudes of mindfulness itself. These are the attitudes that can transform not only difficult situations, but also the texture of your household and your life. When we bring a nonjudgmental attitude of acceptance to each experience—no matter how repulsive to our judge—we come in greater contact with the truth. When we bring kindness and compassion, our shame and sense of failure begin to dissolve. Restored to the invincible vulnerability of the human heart, our potential to heal and to grow together becomes boundless. Nothing can open us to this dimension of our being like the combination of mis-takes and our commitment to recovering with grace.

Summary

Mis-takes are part of life, and encountering them actually nourishes our children. Parenting is not about being perfect, but about keeping our hearts in the right place and leading with humility. Yes, we are responsible for guiding our families with as much wisdom and integrity as possible, but it's not all up to us. Even our missteps "make a music that nobody hears," to borrow again from the words of William Stafford's that opened this chapter. We must trust—despite our judgments to the contrary—that life is unfolding as it should. We may be imperfect, but we are exactly who our child needs.

11.

THE HEART OF MATURITY

How Emotional Intelligence and Resilience Are Grown

The heart is the true inner teacher, the source of inner guidance we all have as our birthright.

—Nirmala, *Living From the Heart*

Much of this book has focused on specific applications and practices; in this chapter, we would like to offer a model of how Mindful Discipline leads to emotional intelligence and resilience in our children. Recall that emotional intelligence and resilience are key aspects of healthy self-discipline that cannot simply be downloaded into our children. Rather, these developmental capacities are grown naturally as long as our children receive the right nourishment: unconditional love, space, mentorship, healthy boundaries, and mis-takes. These five essential elements are most consistently provided through an authoritative style of parenting with mindfulness as its foundation. In this chapter, we will show more specifically how the five essential elements lead to an emotionally intelligent, self-disciplined, and resilient being.

Let's start by looking at how each of these aspects of maturity relate to one another. Recall that *emotional intelligence* can be defined as "the ability to perceive and regulate emotion, and to act in personally and socially intelligent ways." *Self-discipline* is "the process of regulating one's own behavior and acting in accord with one's values and aspirations." And *resilience* is "the ability to persevere, adapt, and bounce back in the face of stress and adversity."

These three qualities are distinct enough to warrant different labels, but they overlap significantly and support one another. Each is necessary for us to reach our full potential in life. We must be able to perceive our inner world of desire and emotion, of what we love and aspire toward. We must be able to regulate that "internal energy" and keep it in a range that allows us to function well. We must also channel all that energy into wise and compassionate action in the world. And when the world challenges us—which it always will—we need to be able to persevere and adapt in the face of stress and adversity. Emotional intelligence, self-discipline, and resilience mutually support one another and allow us to journey through our lives with grace and confidence.

The Self-Disciplined Brain

In this chapter, we want to make two key points. First, our children's brains are innately programmed to develop the capacities of emotional intelligence, self-discipline, and resilience as long as they receive the five forms of nourishment we have been describing in this book. As we discussed in chapter two, discipline is partly a transmission from brain to brain that nourishes growth and development. Each child is born with a particular constitution and temperament. These innate characteristics affect the amount of time she is likely to spend in survive or thrive states, particularly early in her life. But how children are treated by their caregivers can significantly alter these original set points through the growth of regulatory mechanisms in the brain and nervous system. When we attune to our children and meet their needs, they spend more moments in the thrive mode, and they develop the brain regions responsible for shifting them from survive to thrive states on their own during times of stress. This ability to thrive depends on the development of self-regulation and resilience.

The second point we want to make in this chapter is that we, as adult parents, have the ability to intentionally bring mindful awareness practices to the challenging moments of our lives. And, when we choose to bring mindfulness to stressful situations, we actually develop the neural circuitry necessary for us to be better parents. With mindfulness, we become more attuned to our children, ourselves, and the needs of our situations. We become better able to regulate ourselves and our children simultaneously. The intentional use of mindful awareness practices is an act of self-discipline that promotes a healthy brain and healthy relationships. Let's now look at the key brain regions involved in emotional intelligence, self-discipline, and resilience, and how each is impacted by parenting.

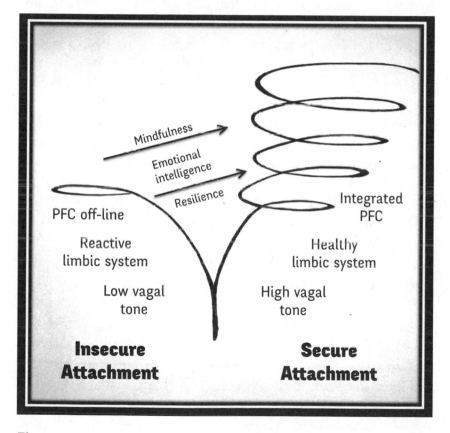

Figure 10: The Fruits of Secure Attachment

Autonomic Nervous System

The autonomic nervous system (ANS) is involved in regulating a variety of basic physiological functions like heart rate, respiration, and blood flow to muscles and organs. The ANS mediates the two main modes we exist in: survive or thrive. In general, think of the survive mode being mediated by the sympathetic branch of the ANS, and the thrive mode as mediated by the parasympathetic branch. The truth is actually far more complex than this, but let's start with the basic model for ease of recall, and expand in complexity from there.

When our perception of a situation—usually unconscious—is that there is a threat or that one of our basic needs is not being met, the sympathetic nervous system becomes activated and increases our heart rate, respiration, and the flow of blood to our muscles to help us work to get our needs met, or to ready us for fight or flight in times of more extreme activation. At the same time, the limbic system becomes more reactive, and our PFC has to work harder to keep us calm and thinking rationally (see below).

On the other hand, when our needs are being met, we perceive the environment as safe, which generally activates the parasympathetic nervous system. This activation calms breathing and heart rate, and allows blood to be shunted to areas responsible for digestion, healing, and growth. The limbic system cools down, allowing the PFC to organize the nervous system more efficiently. A useful way to think of this is that the fulfillment of our basic needs brings our bodies and minds to a state of rest free of the pursuit of getting needs met. In this state, children feel better and are able to learn, function, and mature more easefully.

Again, the actual truth of the ANS is far more complex than the simple survive/sympathetic and thrive/parasympathetic model we've just presented. For one, there are actually two branches of the parasympathetic nervous system: an older evolutionary branch that we share with reptiles and fish—called the *dorsal vagal branch* in humans—and a newer evolutionary branch, the *ventral vagal branch*, that we share with social mammals. The dorsal vagal branch is involved in survival-type reactions, like freezing and fainting, that take hold when the threat is particularly intense. The ventral vagus facilitates our connection to others when we are feeling safe, which is a healthy, thrive-type interaction (Porges 2007). So the parasympathetic nervous system is technically involved in both survive and thrive modes of being, though generally through different branches of the vagus nerve. In this book, we mean *ventral vagus* when we describe thrive-mode parasympathetic activation resulting from the satisfaction of needs.

There are other exceptions to our simplified survive/sympathetic, thrive/parasympathetic model as well. For example, when you and your son are having fun playing on the trampoline together, it is likely that you both have ventral vagal activation (reflecting healthy social engagement) and sympathetic activation (resulting in excitement and increased blood flow to the muscles, lungs, and heart) occurring at the same time. The difference between the sympathetic activation associated with this thrive-mode activity and the sympathetic activation of a survive-mode interaction is this: in the trampoline example, the child's basic needs for relationship are being met. The child is feeling connected to his parent and is thus free from the restless effort in getting that basic need met. That form of "rest" allows the ventral vagal branch of his parasympathetic nervous system to come online and support him in healthy and nourishing social engagement. If the type of interaction involves energy and excitement, as when you're playing together on a trampoline, the sympathetic branch can be recruited without pulling the child into states of reactivity. This is an example of thrive-mode activity that also happens to include some sympathetic nervous system support.

We offer the above examples to be true to the science. But we also believe that, for parenting to be most effective, we can't be lost in our heads thinking about all these details when with our children. This is why we use the simplified survive/thrive model. In moments in which your child is dysregulated, we want you to recognize that their nervous system is telling you "I have a need that's not being met," so that you can help them shift into the thrive mode. By focusing on reading and meeting their need—as opposed to using punishments and rewards to control behavior—you become better able to regulate and teach your child in the moment and help them become self-disciplined over time. (For more of the nuance and specificities of how the ANS is activated in various states of mind, we recommend *The Mindful Brain* by Daniel J. Siegel.)

The takeaway here is that a healthy autonomic nervous system is a fundamental part of healthy self-regulation and self-discipline in life. When infants are routinely protected, cared for, and guided lovingly, they develop what is called *high vagal tone*. The *vagus* is the primary nerve bundle that mediates the parasympathetic effects on the body. When we bring a child's nervous system to rest through attunement and responsiveness to her needs—what researchers call secure attachment—the ventral vagus is activated regularly and becomes stronger, like a muscle (see appendix B, The Basics of Attachment). High vagal tone is a key mediator of healthy self-regulation (Porges 2007).

Limbic System

When it comes to the development of emotional intelligence and resilience, the next important brain region is the limbic system. The limbic system is a very complex region responsible for perception of threat or safety, motivation, generation and regulation of emotion, attention, memory, and social interactions (Siegel and Hartzell 2004). This area assesses if our needs are met enough to shift energy into the thrive mode, or if an unmet need requires a more survival-oriented reaction. The more threat is perceived, the more intense the firing, and the more the sympathetic nervous system (or dorsal vagal parasympathetic system, in the case of freeze and faint reactions) is recruited. A healthy limbic system is able to allow the full repertoire of emotions to flow through it, but is also able to modulate the intensity of activation into a tolerable range so that functioning can continue.

Although some of us are born with a more reactive temperament, this limbic intensity can become modulated over time by attuned and responsive parenting (Lieberman 1993). When we help our children feel safe, when we meet their relational needs to be seen and heard and to feel a sense of belonging, and when we meet their developmental needs for autonomy, competence, and adaptation, their limbic system drives calm down. Children settle into a more natural and harmonious flow where their functioning is optimized and life becomes enjoyable and fulfilling.

When we allow a child to fully experience her emotions—when we communicate to her, "All your desires and feelings are welcome here"— her limbic system remains open and able to fluidly shift from one emotion to another depending on the circumstances. An open limbic system is a prerequisite for emotional intelligence. If a child receives the message that certain emotions are bad or dangerous, she will resort to repression and close her emotional system down in order to feel safe. Unfortunately, repression of emotion is not very precise: it tends to shut down emotion and energy more broadly, causing a variety of physical and mental health problems.

A healthier approach is to allow your child to experience the full range of her emotions, while helping her with appropriate expression. You must learn to distinguish inner experience from outer action, and learn how to work with each skillfully. Helping your child with this distinction supports her in becoming more competent in social interactions, which in turn lowers her limbic reactivity. The more competent she becomes in relationship, the more connected, safe, and fulfilled she feels in her life. The result is a limbic system that is alive and open, but runs a little cooler on the whole.

Prefrontal Cortex (PFC)

The last area of the brain that is responsible for healthy self-discipline is the PFC. The PFC—the CEO of the brain—is intimately interconnected with the limbic system, the ANS, and many other regions of the brain, and plays a primary role in emotional intelligence and resilience. The functions of an integrated middle aspect of the PFC are bodily regulation, emotional balance, downregulation of fear, impulse control and response flexibility, attuned communication, empathy, moral and ethical behavior, self-insight, and intuition (Siegel 2007).

This "know system" can override the limbic system's "go system" reactivity when appropriate (Carter 2010), and the PFC helps us to be more thoughtful and appropriately responsive in the face of challenges. It can stabilize us in the face of discomfort and fear, and help us remain respectful toward others despite being hurt or angry. It can help us remain focused and steadfast toward our long-term goals despite frustration and setbacks. These middle PFC functions are the core of emotional intelligence, resilience, and self-discipline.

The research suggests that these qualities and capacities emerge optimally in the context of secure attachment relationships where the parent takes the lead in protecting, caring for, and guiding the child in a loving way. When the five essential elements of Mindful Discipline are provided, the developing brain is given the experiences it needs to wire up in a healthy, integrated way. And if we as parents continue to support the growth of our own middle PFCs through practices like mindfulness, we will become blessed with the crown jewels of maturity: wisdom, compassion, and integrity. When our PFCs develop optimally, we become embodiments of self-discipline, and the kind of parent every child deserves.

Nourishing the Brain

So now, let's look specifically at how the five essential elements of Mindful Discipline interact with these brain structures, strengthening them and leading to increased emotional intelligence, resilience, and self-discipline.

Unconditional Love

When you love your child unconditionally, her nervous system comes to a state of rest. She feels safe and knows she will be taken care of. She feels that she can be herself and will be accepted for who she is. This strengthens her vagal tone and decreases her limbic reactivity, which increases her capacity for self-regulation and resilience. Her heart will remain open and emotion will flow easefully, creating a strong foundation for the later development of emotional intelligence.

Space

When you give your child space to feel and develop his sense of autonomy, he begins developing his own internal gyroscope of self-regulation. In the absence of excessively tight control, the limbic system reactions of counterwill and collapse become less necessary. Feeling a sense of agency, he pays attention: not only to the outer world of events, but also to the inner world of emotions. Through his feelings of responsibility for his actions, his PFC is exercised like a muscle. Over time, he becomes able to hold more and more complexity, and learn from his mistakes as well as his successes.

Mentorship

When your connection with your child is strong, you can transmit "habits of the heart," giving her an abundance of positive relational experiences. These become a source of resilience and help stabilize her nervous system during stressful encounters. When we help her see emotions as a source of inner guidance and an opportunity for greater connection, we strengthen her PFC capacities for self-insight, empathy, and increasingly ethical behavior.

Healthy Boundaries

Providing healthy boundaries helps your child improve his abilities of impulse control and response flexibility. Instead of being controlled by his limbic system's reactivity, he develops the middle PFC capacity to choose the most appropriate response given the needs of the situation. This is emotional intelligence and self-discipline in action. Through your guidance, he becomes practiced in switching between the upshift and downshift forms of resilience: sticking to it and staying focused when necessary, or accepting reality and sinking into his feelings of disappointment when unable to get his way in the moment.

Mis-takes

The inevitable misattunements provide opportunities for a child to exercise her developing capacity for self-regulation. Through our relational ruptures and repairs, she remains more emotionally open and resilient in the face of discomfort. When we parents respond to the messiness of life with grace and humility, we help our children learn to do the same. Their middle PFC capacities of self-insight and empathy grow and support their ability to maintain rich and intimate relationships throughout their lives.

Summary

The development of emotional intelligence, resilience, and self-discipline unfold naturally when children receive the five essential elements of Mindful Discipline. Through a combination of both love and limits, children develop high vagal tone; a less reactive, more open limbic system; and an integrated PFC. As parents we can continue our own development by engaging in intentional mindfulness practice. Through the cultivation of mindfulness, we find our way back into our inherently wise and loving heart: the best compass for parenting available to us.

12.

EPILOGUE

Who, then, is the doer? Is it the infant who brings her
mother through the veil of self-concern into limitlessness?
Is it the mother, who chooses to hold sacred her infant's
needs and surrender herself? Or is it the One, which
weaves them both through a spiraling path toward
wholeness?

—Vimala McClure, *The Tao of Motherhood*

One definition of discipline is "the creation of greater order."

There is some mysterious force in the universe that opposes entropy,
a dynamic intelligence that moves inexorably toward greater and greater
degrees of wholeness, complexity, and order. Moment by moment, our
children's brains and bodies are being wired up by this intelligence. We
don't see the miraculous process of integration going on beneath the
surface. Instead, we see our child smile back at us for the first time. We
see her light up with pride as she lumbers across the living room into our
outstretched arms. We hear her say things so surprising and unexpect-
edly wise that we stop in our tracks, forced to look more closely at the
little girl we thought we knew. Growing up is the most normal thing in
the world; it just also happens to be one of the most miraculous.

Development has its own momentum. We do not need to be sculptors working day and night, chiseling away at our children as if they were made of stone. We have been asked to tend to our seed-child as a gardener. We engage wholeheartedly, yet also practice nonattachment. We trust the process and the different seasons, and do our best to align our actions with the intelligent unfolding of life.

We parents have been invited to serve this miraculous unfolding—to support our little ones in becoming fully themselves and bringing their gifts to the world. The love we have for our children draws us beyond ourselves moment after moment, day after day. We too are being grown up—made more whole—through every aspect of this relationship: the overwhelm, the sweetness, and sometimes the unbearable heartbreak of loving another so profoundly.

Here is the bottom line: There is no perfect parenting. There is no one right way to do it. This book is, above all, an invitation to trust life, and to welcome mindfulness as your discipline. Each moment you choose to become aware of your breath, of your body, of your child, and of the entire texture of "now," is a moment of mindful presence: the greatest gift you can give your family. We hope that after reading this book you have greater trust in yourself, in your child, and in the intelligence that is living and breathing you, now and always.

Appendices

A

DISCIPLINE AND THE BRAIN

The human brain is composed of approximately a hundred billion neurons and has connections within itself and all through the body. On the physiological level, it is important that your parenting supports the harmonious working of the many different systems of your child's body. When the systems of the body are integrated in any given moment—and especially as they become more integrated over time through the natural processes of development—the experience is one of wholeness, which is the definition of health (Siegel 1999).

One of the most important parts of your child's brain—especially when it comes to self-discipline—is the prefrontal cortex (PFC). The PFC sits right behind the forehead and is considered the CEO of the brain: the seat of executive functioning. This area begins developing early in life, but is not finished developing until *at least* twenty-five years of age. Here is a quick list of the functions of the middle portion of the prefrontal cortex as described by Dr. Dan Siegel (2007):

1. Bodily regulation

2. Emotional balance

3. Downregulation of fear

4. Impulse control and response flexibility

5. Attuned communication

6. Empathy

7. Moral and ethical behavior

8. Self-insight

9. Intuition

If your child's middle PFC wires up in an optimal way, it will support her development into a self-disciplined individual capable of becoming fully herself and sharing her gifts with the world.

Two final points about discipline and the brain:

1. When your child receives the relational nourishment she needs—what researchers call "a secure attachment relationship"—structures involved in self-regulation will wire up in an optimal way. Secure attachment promotes *high vagal tone* (referring to the *vagus*, a cranial nerve bundle that is a key part of the parasympathetic nervous system), and the healthy development of the limbic system (the brain's seat of emotion and memory) and the PFC (the seat of executive function). These key brain regions help the child spend more time in the "thrive" mode, where he or she feels better, functions better, and matures most easefully.

2. Through the practice of mindfulness, you can strengthen and grow your own PFC (rather like strengthening a muscle), leading to wiser and more compassionate parenting—the ultimate gift to your child.

B

THE BASICS OF ATTACHMENT

Attachment theory, in broad terms, is the study of relationship. As social mammals, humans are born with a set of instinctual drives that motivate caregivers and their offspring to seek proximity with one another. Signals are sent back and forth between the pair; when all goes well, the signals are mostly read correctly by the caregiver and the infant's needs are met. The quality of this relationship affects the *firing* of the infant's brain in the moment and the *wiring up* of her or his brain over time. In this way, relationships help shape our brains and their functioning. The quality of attachment is the single most important *modifiable* factor in a child's development.

A caregiver's typical response to her young child—particularly in his time of need—is classified as one of three attachment types: secure attachment, avoidant attachment, and ambivalent attachment (with a fourth category, disorganized attachment, often seen with mentally ill or drug-abusing parents, sometimes added for further descriptive value). These categories were described by researchers who watched parent-child pairs interact in the home and then compared what they saw to infants' responses to separation and reunion in a lab setting. These attachment types are predictive of a whole range of capacities and behavioral strategies in the infant later in life; most useful for our purposes is the fact that secure attachment relationships generally correlate to the list of functions of the PFC listed in appendix A (Siegel and Hartzell 2004). Here is a very brief description of what Mary Ainsworth and others observed (Karen 1994).

In cases of *secure attachment*, in the home, the infant used the parent as a secure base from which to explore and went to her when upset. She appeared confident in her mom's availability and ability to soothe her. The parent appeared to be an available, supportive presence. She offered an optimal level of assistance (enough, but not too much so as to interfere with the child's sense of autonomy), and allowed a wide range of emotional expression. Children raised in such households developed into the most resilient, emotionally intelligent, and self-disciplined individuals.

Avoidant attachment and ambivalent attachment are subtypes of *insecure attachment*. With *avoidant attachment*, in the home, the infant displayed less use of her mother as a secure base, showed random aggression toward her, and was far more clingy and demanding than were securely attached infants. The parent of this attachment dynamic displayed less emotional availability, and was less perceptive and less responsive to her infant's signals. She was also more rejecting, especially when her infant expressed negative emotions or neediness.

With *ambivalent attachment*, in the home, the child was the most overtly anxious, clingy, and demanding of the types tested. The parent was witnessed to be inconsistently available, perceptive, and responsive when the infant needed her. She seemed to frequently have past feelings and memories intrude upon the present moment interactions, and would often inject her own emotional states into the child's current state, rather than attune to and empathize with the child. Children who had these insecure attachment relationships grew up to display less resilience, emotional intelligence, and healthy self-discipline.

For parents, some of the main take-away messages from attachment research are these:

1. Being attuned and responsive to your children, especially when they are in a heightened state of emotion, is optimally supportive of their brain development and their psychoemotional well-being.

2. Children with secure attachment relationships are healthier overall. They show evidence of better self-regulation, emotional

and social intelligence, self-insight, and resilience—functions associated with a well-functioning PFC.

3. If you had a difficult childhood, there are ways to heal and interrupt the transmission of those parenting patterns onto your children. Insecure attachment relationships in childhood can largely be overcome by at least five years within a secure attachment relationship later in life (with an intimate partner, a mentor, or a therapist).

Here are a few other key aspects of attachment within the context of parenting (Neufeld and Maté 2004):

1. Attachment is hierarchical, and the parent-child relationship is asymmetric. What we might call the "attachment brain," located primarily in the limbic system, has two modes: the alpha mode and the dependent mode. The parent is primarily responsible for being in the alpha mode, taking the lead in reading the needs of her child and then providing for those needs. This allows the child to relax into the dependent mode and receive and be fully nourished by the parent.

2. Independence emerges from healthy dependence. Children are like plants, in that pushing and pulling them to grow up faster than the developmental plan is ineffective and often disruptive to healthy growth. The process of individuation unfolds most casefully when we establish a loving hierarchy and cultivate deep roots of healthy dependency.

3. Attachment unfolds in layers. Over time, the ways that we come to feel connected to one another unfold in complexity and character. These can be thought of as roots of attachment, and they provide the foundation for a strong, healthy, vibrant shoot of individuation that we see above the ground (Neufeld 2010).

C

QUALITIES AND CAPACITIES
OF A HEALTHY,
SELF-DISCIPLINED INDIVIDUAL

- Grows beyond self-centeredness and rigid tendencies inherent in early human development and acts in a more flexible and empathic manner

- Able to experience and regulate the whole spectrum of human emotions, and knows how, when, where, and with whom to express herself in an appropriate manner

- Retains an innate curiosity and a deep desire to learn and understand the world around and within him

- Feels free to have her own ideas, feelings, and beliefs, and yet is also aware of the larger social system in which she is embedded

- Is autonomous and feels that he has a strong degree of control and choice in his life, rather than feeling like a victim of circumstances

- Is adaptable and resilient in the face of adversity, and sees challenges as opportunities

- Values and is comfortable with love and intimacy

- Recognizes her capacity for vulnerability as a source of true courage and strength

- Is fulfilled by the simple pleasures of life and does not incessantly seek stimulation and "sugar highs"

- Is spontaneous and intuitive and follows his own creative impulses

- Exhibits a steadfastness and commitment to developing her skills and talents

- Possesses a high degree of self-awareness and the capacity to attune to others

- Feels a sense of meaning and purpose in his life; desires to offer his gifts in the service of others

These are the natural fruits of maturity lying dormant within each child-seed.

D

THE PROMISE AND PERILS OF PRAISE

The self-esteem movement of the past few decades taught that we needed to bolster our children's feelings about themselves by steering them away from challenges and disappointments, and praising them frequently. That approach, while well intended, turned out to be misguided. Encountering challenges and disappointments means that we learn how to deal with them, which builds our resilience and self-confidence more than praise and protection ever could. And, as it happens, the capacity to value oneself is an innate quality, not something we can create in our children, only support or interfere with. It is easily preserved when we provide the five essential elements of Mindful Discipline to our children.

The discrediting of the self-esteem model has left many parents uncertain about praise—will we harm our children with our praise? But not all praise is equal, and not all praise is harmful. There is sugarcoated, manipulative praise, where the parent is using praise to get some result—trying to increase a particular behavior or boost the child's self-esteem, for example. And there is sincere, celebrating-with praise, where the "praise" is simply enjoying your child's achievements together, with no other agenda. The former pushes the psyche toward our survival mode, where self-image is fragile (either grandiose or collapsed). The latter is merely a supportive aspect of healthy relationship. Sincere, celebrating-with praise—"That's awesome, Kyla. I am happy for you"—preserves autonomy, amplifies a child's joy in becoming more competent, and deepens connection: each of these are aspects of our thriving mode.

Liberal use of sugarcoated, manipulative praise has been shown to decrease perceived autonomy, make children less persistent, and lower their courage in tackling more challenging material. These children also spend more time on image maintenance and on tearing down others. Children exposed to liberal praise were found to be more likely to drop classes in college to avoid a mediocre grade and have a harder time picking a major; they are afraid to commit to something for fear of failing (Bronson and Merryman 2009).

Another distinction in the praise literature has been made between promoting a "fixed" versus a "growth" mindset. Professor of psychology at Stanford University Carol Dweck (discussed in Pink 2009) found that when you praise children for fixed traits like intelligence—"You are so smart"—they are much less likely to try a harder test the next time. Fewer than 50 percent of the "smart" children chose the more challenging test after being praised. Compare this to children praised for their effort—"You must have really worked hard"—who chose the more challenging test 90 percent of the time. This growth-mindset feedback increased their courage and enthusiasm. Not only that, the type of feedback children received actually impacted their *performance* as well. Dweck gave a second round of tests to both groups of children; this time an impossible test that all children failed. Then, to see how each group would cope with their "failure," she gave a third test, equal in difficulty to the first. The scores in the fixed-image praise group went down by 20 percent, while the scores in the growth-mindset feedback group went up by 30 percent. Teaching children that they are in a sense a *process*, and that they have some measure of control over their success—in the effort they put in and the strategies they choose—increases their resilience and their performance (Bronson and Merryman 2009).

So, if you must praise...

1. Be sincere. If you blow smoke too much, children will catch on soon enough and then come to not trust anything you say (even when it is true).

2. Praise in private. Giving feedback in front of other people will push the psyche over toward image orientation (a survival-oriented strategy) rather than allowing the child to focus on learning (a characteristic of thriving).

3. Praise effort and strategy. "Way to stick to it" is more beneficial than "You are really smart."

4. Be specific rather than general. "I like the way you shaded that part of the house. It looks more three-dimensional like that," rather than "Great drawing!" (Pink 2009)

SUGGESTED READING

Everyday Blessings by Jon and Myla Kabat-Zinn

Wherever You Go, There You Are by Jon Kabat-Zinn

Hold on to your Kids by Gordon Neufeld and Gabor Maté

Parenting from the Inside Out by Dan Siegel and Mary Hartzell

The Tao of Motherhood by Vimala McClure

Raising Happiness by Christine Carter

The Art of Forgiveness, Lovingkindness, and Peace by Jack Kornfield

The Self-Esteem Trap by Polly Young-Eisendrath

Unconditional Parenting by Alfie Kohn

Buddha's Brain by Rick Hanson

The Whole-Brain Child by Daniel Siegel and Tina Bryson

Mindful Motherhood by Cassandra Vieten

Raising an Emotionally Intelligent Child by John Gottman

Positive Discipline by Jane Nelsen

REFERENCES

Almaas, A. H. 1987. *Diamond Heart Book 1.* Boston: Shambhala Publications.

Bate, John. 1888. *Six Thousand Illustrations of Moral and Religious Truths: Consisting of Definitions, Metaphors, Similes, Emblems, Contrasts, Analogies, Statistics, Synonyms, Anecdotes, Etc.* London: Jarrold and Sons.

Bronson, Po, and Ashley Merryman. 2009. *NurtureShock.* New York: Hachette.

Calhoun, Adele. 2011. *Invitations from God.* Downers Grove, IL: Intervarsity Press.

Canfield, Jack. 2000. *Chicken Soup for the Expectant Mother's Soul.* Deerfield Beach, FL: Health Communications.

Carter, Christine. 2010. *Raising Happiness.* New York: Ballantine Books.

Chodron, Pema. 1994. *Start Where You Are.* Boston: Shambhala Publications.

Chodron, Pema. 2009. *Unconditional Confidence.* Audio CD. Louisville, CO: Sounds True, Inc.

Collopy, Michael. 2002. *Architects of Peace: Visions of Hope in Words and Images.* Novato, CA: New World Library.

Cotton, Kathleen. 1995. "Developing Empathy in Children and Youth." Educations Northwest School Improvement Research Series Close-Up No. 13. http://educationnorthwest.org/webfm_send/556.

Epstein, Mark. 1998. *Going to Pieces Without Falling Apart.* New York: Broadway Books.

Frank, Anne. 1952. *The Diary of a Young Girl.* New York: Bantam Books.

Frankl, Viktor. 1992. *Man's Search for Meaning.* Boston: Beacon Press.

Gamper, Carmen. 2011. *The Sacred Child Companion: Handbook for Child-Centered Learning.* San Rafael, CA: New Learning Culture.

Gibran, Kahlil. 1923. *The Prophet.* New York: Alfred A. Knopf, Inc.

Gladwell, Malcolm. 2008. *Outliers.* New York: Back Bay Books.

Goleman, Daniel. 1995. *Emotional Intelligence.* New York: Bantam Books.

Gottman, John. 1997. *Raising an Emotionally Intelligent Child.* New York: Simon and Schuster.

Grolnick, Wendy S. 2009. *The Psychology of Parental Control.* New York: Psychology Press.

Hafiz. 1999. *The Gift,* translated by Daniel Ladinsky. Harmondsworth, UK: Penguin.

Hanh, Thich Nhat. 1995. *Living Buddha, Living Christ.* New York: Riverhead Books.

Johnson, Sara, Anna W. Riley, Douglas A. Granger, and Jenna Riis. 2013. The Science of Early Life Toxic Stress for Pediatric Practice and Advocacy. *Pediatrics* 131(2): 319–27.

Kabat-Zinn, Jon. 1994. *Wherever You Go, There You Are.* New York: Hyperion.

Kabat-Zinn, Jon, and Myla Kabat-Zinn. 1997. *Everyday Blessings.* New York: Hyperion.

Karen, Robert. 1994. *Becoming Attached: First Relationsips and How They Shape Our Capacity To Love.* New York: Warner Books.

King, Martin Luther, Jr. 1967. "Where Do We Go From Here?" Address to the Southern Christian Leadership Conference, August 16.

Kohn, Alfie. 2005. *Unconditional Parenting.* New York: Atria Books.

Kohn, Alfie. 2001. "Five Reasons to Stop Saying 'Good Job!'" *Young Children* 56(5): 24–8.

Kornfield, Jack. 2002. *The Art of Forgiveness, Lovingkindness, and Peace.* New York: Bantam Books.

Krishnamurti, Jiddu. 1992. *On Relationship.* New York: HarperCollins.

Lao Tzu. 1995. *Tao Te Ching,* translated by Stephen Mitchell. New York: HarperCollins.

Lieberman, Alicia F. 1993. *The Emotional Life of the Toddler.* New York: The Free Press.

Lieberman, Matthew D. 2013. *Social: Why Our Brains Are Wired to Connect.* New York: Crown Publishers.

McClure, Vimala. 1991. *The Tao of Motherhood.* Willow Springs, MO: Nucleus Publications.

Meade, Michael, Malidowia Some, Luis Rodriguez, Jack Kornfield, and Orland Bishop. n.d. *The Genius of Mentoring.* Audio CD. Seattle: Mosaic Audio.

Minowa, Craig. 2008. "No One Said It Would Be Easy," song from album *Feel Good Ghosts.* Viroqua, WI: Earthology Records.

Nelsen, Jane. 1981. *Positive Discipline.* Fair Oaks, CA: Sunrise Press.

Neufeld, Gordon, and Gabor Maté. 2004. *Hold on to Your Kids.* New York: Ballantine Books.

Neufeld, Gordon. 2010. *Neufeld Intensive Level One.* Vancouver: Neufeld Institute.

Nirmala. 2008. *Living From the Heart.* Sedona, AZ: Endless Satsang Foundation.

Palmer, Wendy. 1994. *The Intuitive Body.* Berkeley: North Atlantic Books.

Piaget, Jean. 1997. *The Moral Judgment of the Child.* New York: Simon and Schuster.

Pink, Daniel H. 2009. *Drive: The Surprising Truth About What Motivates Us.* New York: Riverhead Books.

Porges, Stephen W. 2007. "The Polyvagal Perspective." *Biological Psychology* 74 (2): 116–43.

Rilke, Rainer Maria. 1969. *Letters of Rainer Maria Rilke, 1910–1926*, translated by Jane Bannard Greene and M. D. Herter Norton. New York: W. W. Norton.

Rilke, Rainer Maria. 1986. *Letters to a Young Poet*, translated by Stephen Mitchell. New York: Vintage.

Shapiro, Shauna, and Linda Carlson. 2009. *The Art and Science of Mindfulness*. Washington, DC: American Psychological Association.

Siegel, Daniel, and Tina Bryson. 2011. *The Whole-Brain Child*. New York: Delacorte Press.

Siegel, Daniel, and Mary Hartzell. 2004. *Parenting From the Inside Out*. New York: Penguin.

Siegel, Daniel. 2007. *The Mindful Brain*. New York: W. W. Norton.

Stafford, William. 1998. *The Way It Is*. Minneapolis, MN: Graywolf Press.

Swimme, Brian. 1996. *The Hidden Heart of the Cosmos*. New York: Orbis Books.

Wallace, B. Alan. 2006. *The Attention Revolution: Unlocking the Power of the Focused Mind*. Somerville, MA: Wisdom Publications.

Wallin, David J. 2007. *Attachment in Psychotherapy*. New York: Guilford Press.

Wilber, Ken. 2000. *Integral Psychology*. Boston: Shambhala Publications.

Williamson, Marianne. 1992. *A Return to Love*. New York: HarperCollins.

Winnicott, D. W. 1964. *The Child, the Family, and the Outside World*. New York: Perseus Publishing.

Wipfler, Patty. 2006. *Listening to Children*. Palo Alto, CA: Hand in Hand Parenting.

Young-Eisendrath, Polly. 2008. *The Self-Esteem Trap: Raising Confident and Compassionate Kids in an Age of Self-Importance*. New York: Little, Brown and Company.

Shauna Shapiro, PhD, is a professor at Santa Clara University, a clinical psychologist, an internationally recognized expert in mindfulness, and a mother. With twenty years of meditation experience studying in Thailand and Nepal, as well as in the West, Shapiro brings an embodied sense of mindfulness to her scientific work. She has published over one hundred journal articles and chapters, and coauthored the critically acclaimed book, *The Art and Science of Mindfulness*. Shapiro is the recipient of the American Council of Learned Societies teaching award, acknowledging her outstanding contributions to education, and has been invited to lecture for the King of Thailand, the Danish government, and the World Council for Psychotherapy in Beijing, China. Her work has been featured in *Wired, USA Today, Oxygen, The Yoga Journal,* and the *American Psychologist*. Shapiro lives in Mill Valley, California, with her eight-year-old son, Jackson.

Chris White, MD, is a board-certified pediatrician, parent educator, certified life coach, and father. He is the creator and director of Essential Parenting, an organization that supports the psycho-emotional development of children and their parents. His writing has been featured in *Pathways to Family Wellness* and the PBS series' *This Emotional Life* blog. White lives with his two boys, Kai and Bodhi, and the love of his life, Kari, in the San Francisco Bay Area.

Foreword writer **Christine Carter, PhD**, is a happiness expert, sociologist, and the author of *Raising Happiness: 10 Simple Steps for More Joyful Kids and Happier Parents*. Carter has helped thousands of people find more joy in their lives through her books, online classes, coaching, and speaking engagements. She teaches happiness classes online throughout the year to a global audience on her website www.christinecarter.com.

Foreword writer **Dean Ornish, MD**, is the founder and president of the non-profit Preventive Medicine Research Institute and clinical professor of medicine at the University of California, San Francisco. Ornish received his MD from the Baylor College of Medicine, was a clinical fellow in medicine at Harvard Medical School, and completed an internship and residency in internal medicine at the Massachusetts General Hospital. He is the author of six books, all national bestsellers, including: *Dr. Dean Ornish's Program for Reversing Heart Disease*; *Eat More, Weigh Less*; *Love and Survival*; and his most recent book, *The Spectrum*.

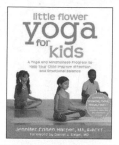